John Armor Bingham

Trial of the Conspirators, for the Assassination of President Lincoln, etc.

Argument of John A. Bingham in Reply to the Arguments of the several Counsel for Mary E. Surratt, David E. Herold, etc.

John Armor Bingham

Trial of the Conspirators, for the Assassination of President Lincoln, etc.
Argument of John A. Bingham in Reply to the Arguments of the several Counsel for Mary E. Surratt, David E. Herold, etc.

ISBN/EAN: 9783337192358

Printed in Europe, USA, Canada, Australia, Japan

Cover: Foto ©ninafisch / pixelio.de

More available books at **www.hansebooks.com**

TRIAL OF THE CONSPIRATORS FOR THE ASSASSINATION OF
PRESIDENT LINCOLN, &c.

ARGUMENT

OF

JOHN A. BINGHAM,

SPECIAL JUDGE ADVOCATE,

IN REPLY TO THE

ARGUMENTS OF THE SEVERAL COUNSEL FOR MARY E. SURRATT,
DAVID E. HEROLD, LEWIS PAYNE, GEORGE A. ATZERODT,
MICHAEL O'LAUGHLIN, SAMUEL A. MUDD, EDWARD
SPANGLER, AND SAMUEL ARNOLD, CHARGED
WITH CONSPIRACY AND THE MURDER
OF ABRAHAM LINCOLN, LATE
PRESIDENT OF THE
UNITED STATES.

**Delivered June 27 and 28, 1865, before the Military
Commission, Washington, D. C.**

WASHINGTON:
GOVERNMENT PRINTING OFFICE.
1865.

ARGUMENT

OF

JOHN A. BINGHAM,

SPECIAL JUDGE ADVOCATE

IN REPLY TO

THE SEVERAL ARGUMENTS IN DEFENCE OF MARY E. SURRATT AND OTHERS, CHARGED WITH CONSPIRACY AND THE MURDER OF ABRAHAM LINCOLN, LATE PRESIDENT OF THE UNITED STATES, &c.

MAY IT PLEASE THE COURT: The conspiracy here charged and specified, and the acts alleged to have been committed in pursuance thereof, and with the intent laid, constitute a crime the atrocity of which has sent a shudder through the civilized world. All that was agreed upon and attempted by the alleged inciters and instigators of this crime constitutes a combination of atrocities with scarcely a parallel in the annals of the human race. Whether the prisoners at your bar are guilty of the conspiracy and the acts alleged to have been done in pursuance thereof, as set forth in the charge and specification, is a question the determination of which rests solely with this honorable court, and in passing upon which this court are the sole judges of the law and the fact.

In presenting my views upon the questions of law raised by the several counsel for the defence, and also on the testimony adduced for and against the accused, I desire to be just to them, just to you, just to my country, and just to my own convictions. The issue joined involves the highest interests of the accused, and, in my judgment, the highest interests of the whole people of the United States.

It is a matter of great moment to all the people of this country that the prisoners at your bar be lawfully tried and lawfully convicted or acquitted. A wrongful and illegal conviction or a wrongful and illegal acquittal upon this dread issue would impair somewhat the security of every man's life, and shake the stability of the republic.

The crime charged and specified upon your record is not simply the crime of murdering a human being, but it is the crime of killing and murdering on the 14th day of April, A. D. 1865, within the military department of Washington and the intrenched lines thereof, Abraham Lincoln, then President of the United States, and commander-in-chief of the army and navy thereof; and then and there assaulting, with intent to kill and murder, William H. Seward, then Secretary of State of the United States; and then and there lying in wait to kill and murder Andrew Johnson, then Vice President of the United States, and Ulysses S. Grant, then lieutenant general and in command of the armies of the United States, in pursuance of a treasonable conspiracy entered into by the accused with one John Wilkes Booth, and John H. Surratt, upon the instigation of Jefferson Davis, Jacob Thompson, and George N. Sanders and others, with intent thereby to aid the existing rebellion and subvert the Constitution and laws of the United States.

The rebellion, in aid of which this conspiracy was formed and this great public crime committed, was prosecuted for the vindication of no right, for the redress of no wrong, but was itself simply a criminal conspiracy and gigantic assassination. In resisting and crushing this rebellion the American people take no step backward, and cast no reproach upon their past history. That people now, as ever, proclaim the self-evident truth that whenever government becomes subversive of the ends of its creation, it is the right and duty of the people to alter or abolish it; but during these four years of conflict they have as clearly proclaimed, as was their right and duty, both by law and by arms, that the government of their own choice, humanely and wisely administered, oppressive of none and just to all, shall not be overthrown by privy conspiracy or armed rebellion.

What wrong had this government or any of its duly constituted agents done to any of the guilty actors in this atrocious rebellion? They themselves being witnesses, the government which they assailed had done no act, and attempted no act, injurious to them, or in any sense violative of their rights as citizens and men; and yet for four years, without cause of complaint or colorable excuse, the inciters and instigators of the conspiracy charged upon your record have, by armed rebellion, resisted the lawful authority of the government, and attempted by force of arms to blot the republic from the map of nations. Now that their battalions of treason are broken and flying before the victorious legions of the republic, the chief traitors in this great crime against your government secretly conspire with their hired confederates to achieve by assassination, if possible, what they have in vain attempted by wager of battle—the overthrow of the government of the United States and the subversion of its Constitution and laws. It is for this secret conspiracy in the interest of the rebellion, formed at the instigation of the chiefs in that rebellion, and in pursuance of which the acts charged and specified are alleged to have been done and with the intent laid, that the accused are upon trial.

The government in preferring this charge does not indict the whole people of any State or section, but only the alleged parties to this unnatural and atrocious conspiracy and crime. The President of the United States, in the discharge of his duty as commander-in-chief of the army, and by virtue of the power vested in him by the Constitution and laws of the United States, has constituted you a military court, to hear and determine the issue joined against the accused, and has constituted you a court for no other purpose whatever. To this charge and specification the defendants have pleaded, first, that this court has no jurisdiction in the premises; and, second, not guilty. As the court has already overruled the plea to the jurisdiction, it would be passed over in silence by me but for the fact, that a grave and elaborate argument has been made by counsel for the accused, not only to show the want of jurisdiction, but to arraign the President of the United States before the country and the world as a usurper of power over the lives and the liberties of the prisoners. Denying the authority of the President to constitute this commission is an averment that this tribunal is not a court of justice, has no legal existence, and therefore no power to hear and determine the issue joined. The learned counsel for the accused, when they make this averment by way of argument, owe it to themselves and to their country to show how the President could otherwise lawfully and efficiently discharge the duty enjoined upon him by his oath to protect, preserve, and defend the Constitution of the United States, and to take care that the laws be faithfully executed.

An existing rebellion is alleged and not denied. It is charged that in aid of this existing rebellion a conspiracy was entered into by the accused, incited and instigated thereto by the chiefs of this rebellion, to kill and murder the executive officers of the government, and the commander of the armies of the United States, and that this conspiracy was partly executed by the murder of Abraham Lincoln, and by a murderous assault upon the Secretary of State; and counsel reply, by elaborate argument, that although the facts be as charged, though the conspirators be numerous and at large, able and eager to complete the horrid work of assassination already begun within your military encampment, yet the successor of your murdered President is a usurper if he attempts by military force and martial law, as commander-in-chief, to prevent the consummation of this traitorous conspiracy in aid of this treasonable rebellion. The civil courts, say the counsel, are open in the District. I answer, they are closed throughout half the republic, and were only open in this District on the day of this confederation and conspiracy, on the day of the traitorous assassination of your President, and are only open at this hour, by force of the bayonet. Does any man suppose that if the military forces which garrison the intrenchments of your capital, fifty thousand strong, were all withdrawn, the rebel bands who this day infest the mountain passes in your vicinity would allow this court, or any court, to remain open in this District for the trial of these their confederates, or would permit your executive officers to discharge the trust committed to them, for twenty-four hours?

At the time this conspiracy was entered into, and when this court was convened and entered upon this trial, the country was in a state of civil war. An army of insurrectionists have, since this trial begun, shed the blood of Union soldiers in battle. The conspirator, by whose hand his co-conspirators, whether present or absent, jointly murdered the President on the 14th of last April, could not be and was not arrested upon civil process, but was pursued by the military power of the government, captured, and slain. Was this an act of usurpation?—a violation of the right guaranteed to that fleeing assassin by the very Constitution against which and for the subversion of which he had conspired and murdered the President? Who in all this land is bold enough or base enough to assert it?

I would be glad to know by what law the President, by a military force, acting only upon his military orders, is justified in pursuing, arresting, and killing one of these conspirators, and is condemned for arresting in like manner, and by his order subjecting to trial, according to the laws of war, any or all of the other parties to this same damnable conspiracy and crime, by a military tribunal of justice—a tribunal, I may be pardoned for saying, whose integrity and impartiality are above suspicion, and pass unchallenged even by the accused themselves.

The argument against the jurisdiction of this court rests upon the assumption that even in time of insurrection and civil war, no crimes are cognizable and punishable by military commission or court-martial, save crimes committed in the military or naval service of the United States, or in the militia of the several States when called into the actual service of the United States. But that is not all the argument: it affirms that under this plea to the jurisdiction, the accused have the right to demand that this court shall decide that it is not a judicial tribunal and has no legal existence.

This is a most extraordinary proposition—that the President, under the Constitution and laws of the United States, was not only not authorized but absolutely forbidden to constitute this court for the trial of the accused, and, therefore, the act of the President is void, and the gentlemen who compose the tribunal without judicial authority or power, and are not in fact or in law a court.

That I do not misstate what is claimed and attempted to be established on behalf of the accused, I ask the attention of the court to the following as the gentleman's (Mr. Johnson's) propositions:

That Congress has not authorized, and, under the Constitution, cannot authorize the appointment of this commission.

That this commission has, "as a court, no legal existence or authority," because the President, who alone appointed the commission, has no such power.

That his act "is a mere nullity—the usurpation of a power not vested in the Executive, and conferring no authority upon you."

We have had no common exhibition of law learning in this Defence, prepared by a Senator of the United States; but with all his experience, and all his learning, and acknowledged ability, he has failed, utterly failed, to show how a tribunal constituted and sworn, as this has been, to duly try and determine the charge and specification against the accused, and by its commission not authorized to hear or determine any other issues whatever, can rightfully entertain, or can by any possibility pass upon, the proposition presented by this argument of the gentleman for its consideration.

The members of this court are officers in the army of the United States, and by order of the President, as Commander-in-Chief, are required to discharge this duty, and are authorized in this capacity to discharge no other duty, to exercise no other judicial power. Of course, if the commission of the President constitutes this a court for the trial of this case only, as such court it is competent to decide all questions of law and fact arising in the trial of the case. But this court has no power, as a court, to declare the authority by which it was constituted null and void, and the act of the

President a mere nullity, a usurpation. Has it been shown by the learned gentleman, who demands that this court shall so decide, that officers of the army may lawfully and constitutionally question in this manner the orders of their Commander-in-Chief, disobey, set them aside, and declare them a nullity and a usurpation? Even if it be conceded that the officers thus detailed by order of the Commander-in-Chief may question and utterly disregard his order and set aside his authority, is it possible, in the nature of things, that any body of men, constituted and qualified as a tribunal of justice, can sit in judgment upon the proposition that they are not a court for any purpose, and finally decide judicially, as a court, that the government which appointed them was without authority? Why not crown the absurdity of this proposition by asking the several members of this court to determine that they are not men—living, intelligent, responsible men! This would be no more irrational than the question upon which they are asked to pass. How can any sensible man entertain it? Before he begins to reason upon the proposition he must take for granted, and therefore decide in advance, the very question in dispute, to wit, his actual existence.

So with the question presented in this remarkable argument for the defence: before this court can enter upon the inquiry of the want of authority in the President to constitute them a court, they must take for granted and decide the very point in issue, that the President had the authority, and that they are in law and in fact a judicial tribunal; and having assumed this, they are gravely asked, as such judicial tribunal, to finally and solemnly decide and declare that they are not in fact or in law a judicial tribunal, but a mere nullity and nonentity. A most lame and impotent conclusion!

As the learned counsel seems to have great reverence for judicial authority, and requires precedent for every opinion, I may be pardoned for saying that the objection which I urge, against the possibility of any judicial tribunal, after being officially qualified as such, entertaining, much less judicially deciding, the proposition that it has no legal existence as a court, and that the appointment was a usurpation and without authority of law, has been solemnly ruled by the Supreme Court of the United States.

That court say: "The acceptance of the judicial office is a recognition of the *authority* from which it is derived. If a court should enter upon the inquiry (whether the *authority* of the government which established it existed,) and should come to the conclusion that the government under which it acted had been put aside, it would cease to be a court and be *incapable* of pronouncing a judicial decision upon the question it undertook to try. If it decides at all, as a court, it necessarily affirms the existence and *authority* of the government under which it is exercising judicial power."—(Luther *vs.* Borden, 7 Howard, 40.)

That is the very question raised by the learned gentleman in his argument—that there was no *authority* in the President, by whose act alone this tribunal was constituted, to vest it with judicial power to try this issue ; and by the order upon your record, as has already been shown, if you have no power to try this issue for want of authority in the Commander-in-Chief to constitute you a court, you are no court, and have no power to try any issue, because his order limits you to this issue, and this alone.

It requires no very profound legal attainments to apply the ruling of the highest judicial tribunal of this country, just cited, to the point raised, not by the pleadings, but by the argument. This court exists as a judicial tribunal by authority only of the President of the United States ; the acceptance of the office is an acknowledgment of the validity of the authority conferring it, and if the President had no authority to order, direct, and constitute this court to try the accused, and, as is claimed, did, in so constituting it, perform an unconstitutional and illegal act, it necessarily results that the order of the President is void and of no effect; that the order did not and could not constitute this a tribunal of justice, and therefore its members are incapable of pronouncing a judicial decision upon the question presented.

There is a marked distinction between the question here presented and that raised by a plea to the jurisdiction of a tribunal whose existence as a court is neither questioned nor denied. Here it is argued, through many pages, by a learned Senator, and a distinguished lawyer, that the order of the President, by whose authority alone this court is constituted a tribunal of military justice, is unlawful; if unlawful it is void and of no effect, and has created no court; therefore this body, not being a court, can have no more power as a court to decide any question whatever than have its individual members power to decide that they as men do not in fact exist.

It is a maxim of the common law—the perfection of human reason— that what is impossible the law requires of no man.

How can it be possible that a judicial tribunal can decide the question that it does not exist, any more than that a rational man can decide that he does not exist?

The absurdity of the proposition so elaborately urged upon the consideration of this court cannot be saved from the ridicule and contempt of sensible men by the pretence that the court is not asked judicially to decide that it is not a court, but only that it has no jurisdiction; for it is a fact not to be denied that the whole argument for the defence on this point is that the President had not the lawful authority to issue the order by which alone this court is constituted, and that the order for its creation is null and void.

Gentlemen might as well ask the Supreme Court of the United States upon a plea to the jurisdiction to decide, as a court, that the President had no lawful authority to nominate the judges thereof severally to the Senate, and that the Senate had no lawful authority to advise and consent to their appointment, as to ask this court to decide, as a court, that the order of the President of the United States constituting it a tribunal for the sole purpose of this trial was not only without authority of law, but against and in violation of law. If this court is not a lawful tribunal, it has no existence, and can no more speak as a court than the dead, much less pronounce the judgment required at its hands—that it is not a court, and that the President of the United States, in constituting it such to try the question upon the charge and specification preferred, has transcended his authority, and violated his oath of office.

Before passing from the consideration of the proposition of the learned senator, that this is not a court, it is fit that I should notice that another of the counsel for the accused (Mr. Ewing) has also advanced the same opinion, certainly with more directness and candor, and without any qualification. His statement is, "You," gentlemen, "are no court under the Constitution." This remark of the gentleman cannot fail to excite surprise, when it is remembered that the gentleman, not many months since, was a general in the service of the country, and as such in his department in the west proclaimed and enforced martial law by the constitution of military tribunals for the trial of citizens not in the land or naval forces, but who were guilty of military offences, for which he deemed them justly punishable before military courts, and accordingly he punished them. Is the gentleman quite sure, when that account comes to be rendered for these alleged unconstitutional assumptions of power, that he will not have to answer for more of these alleged violations of the rights of citizens by illegal arrests, convictions, and executions, than any of the members of this court? In support of his opinion that this is no court, the gentleman cites the 3d article of the Constitution, which provides "that the judicial power of the United States shall be vested in one supreme court, and such inferior courts as Congress may establish," the judges whereof "shall hold their offices during good behavior."

It is a sufficient answer to say to the gentleman, that the power of this government to try and punish military offences by military tribunals is no part of the "judicial power of the United States," under the 3d article of the Constitution, but a power conferred by the 8th section of the 1st article, and so it has been ruled by the Supreme Court in *Dyres* vs. *Hoover*, 20 Howard, 78. If this power is so conferred by the 8th section, a military court authorized by Congress, and constituted as this has been, to try all persons for military crimes in time of war, though not exercising "the judicial power" provided for in the 3d article, is nevertheless a court as constitutional as the Supreme Court itself. The gentleman admits this to the extent of the trial by courts-martial of persons in the military or naval service, and by admitting it he gives up the point. There is no *express* grant for any such tribunal, and the power to establish such a court, therefore, is *implied* from the provisions of the 8th section, 1st article, that "Congress shall have power to provide and maintain a navy," and also "to make rules for the government of the land and naval forces." From these grants the Supreme Court infer the power to establish courts-martial, and from the grants in the same 8th section, as I shall notice hereafter, that "Congress shall have power to declare war," and "to pass all laws necessary and proper to carry this and all other powers into effect," it is necessarily implied that in time of war Congress may authorize military commissions, to try all crimes committed in aid of the public enemy, as such tribunals are *necessary* to give effect to the power to make war and suppress insurrection.

Inasmuch as the gentleman (Gen. Ewing,) for whom, personally, I have a high regard as the military commander of a western department, made a liberal exercise, under the order of the Commander-in-Chief of the army, of this power to arrest and try military offenders not in the land or naval forces of the United States, and inflicted upon them, as I am informed, the extreme penalty of the law, by virtue of his military jurisdiction, I wish to know whether he proposes, by his proclamation of the personal responsibility awaiting all such usurpations of judicial authority, that he himself shall be subjected to the same stern judgment which he invokes against others—that, in short, he shall be drawn and quartered for inflicting the extreme penalties of the law upon citizens of the United States in violation of the Constitution and laws of his country? I trust that his error of judgment in pronouncing this military jurisdiction a usurpation and violation of the Constitution may not rise up in judgment to condemn him, and that he may never be subjected to pains and penalties for having done his duty heretofore in exercising this rightful authority, and in bringing to judgment those who conspired against the lives and liberties of the people.

Here I might leave this question, committing it to the charitable speeches of men, but for the fact that the learned counsel has been more careful in his extraordinary argument to denounce the President as a usurper than to show how the court could possibly decide that it has no judicial existence, and yet that it has judicial existence.

A representative of the people and of the rights of the people before this court, by the appointment of the President, and which appointment was neither sought by me nor desired, I cannot allow all that has here been said by way of denunciation of the murdered President and his successor to pass unnoticed. This has been made the occasion by the learned counsel, Mr. Johnson, to volunteer, not to defend the accused, Mary E. Surratt, not to make a judicial argument in her behalf, but to make a political harangue, a partisan speech against his government and country, and thereby swell the cry of the armed legions of sedition and rebellion that but yesterday shook the heavens with their infernal enginery of treason and filled the habitations of the people with death. As the law forbids a senator of the United States to receive compensation, or fee, for defending, in cases before civil or military commissions, the gentleman volunteers to make a speech before this court, in which he denounces the action of the Executive Department in proclaiming and executing martial law against rebels in arms, their aiders and abettors, as a usurpation and a tyranny. I deem it my duty to reply to this denunciation, not for the purpose of presenting thereby any question for the decision of this court, for I have shown that the argument of the gentleman presents no question for its decision as a court, but to repel, as far as I may be able, the unjust aspersion attempted to be cast upon the memory of our dead President, and upon the official conduct of his successor.

I propose now to answer fully all that the gentleman (Mr. Johnson) has said of the want of jurisdiction in this court, and of the alleged usurpation and tyranny of the Executive, that the enlightened public opinion to which he appeals may decide whether all this denunciation is just—whether indeed conspiring against the whole people, and confederation and agreement in aid of insurrection to murder all the executive officers of the government, cannot be checked or arrested by the Executive power. Let the people decide this question ; and in doing so, let them pass upon the action of the senator as well as upon the action of those whom he so arrogantly arraigns. His plea in behalf of an expiring and shattered rebellion is a fit subject for public consideration and for public condemnation.

Let that people also note, that while the learned gentleman, (Mr. Johnson,) as a volunteer, without pay, thus condemns as a usurpation the means employed so effectually to suppress this gigantic insurrection, the New York News, whose proprietor, Benjamin Wood, is shown by the testimony upon your record to have received from the agents of the rebellion twenty-five thousand dollars, rushes into the lists to champion the cause of the rebellion, its aiders and abettors, by following to the letter his colleague, (Mr. Johnson,) and with greater plainness of speech, and a fervor intensified, doubtless, by the twenty-five thousand dollars received, and the hope of more, denounces the court as a usurpation and threatens the members with the consequences !

The argument of the gentleman to which the court has listened so patiently and so long is but an attempt to show that it is unconstitutional for the government of the United States to arrest upon military order and try before military tribunals and punish upon conviction, in accordance with the laws of war and the usages of nations, all criminal offenders acting in aid of the existing rebellion. It does seem to me that the speech in its tone and temper is the same as that which the country has heard for the last four years uttered by the armed rebels themselves and by their apologists, averring that it was unconstitutional for the government of the United States to defend by arms its own rightful authority and the supremacy of its laws.

It is as clearly the right of the republic to live and to defend its life until it forfeits that right by crime, as it is the right of the individual to live so long as God gives him life, unless he forfeits that right by crime. I make no argument to support this proposition. Who is there here or elsewhere to cast the reproach upon my country that for her crimes she must die ? Youngest born of the nations ! is she not immortal by all the dread memories of the past—by that sublime and voluntary sacrifice of the present, in which the bravest and noblest of her sons have laid down their lives that she might live, giving their serene brows to the dust of the grave, and lifting their hands for the last time amidst the consuming fires of battle! I assume, for the purposes of this argument, that self-defence is as clearly the right of nations as it is the acknowledged right of men, and that the American people may do in the defence and maintenance of their own rightful authority against organized armed rebels, their aiders and abettors, whatever free and independent nations anywhere upon this globe, in time of war, may of right do.

All this is substantially denied by the gentleman in the remarkable argument which he has here made. There is nothing further from my purpose than to do injustice to the learned gentleman or to his elaborate and ingenious argument. To justify what I have already said, I may be permitted here to remind the court that nothing is said by the counsel touching the conduct of the accused, Mary E. Surratt, as shown by the testimony; that he makes confession at the end of his arraignment of the government and country, that he has not made such argument, and that he leaves it to be made by her other counsel. He does take care, however, to arraign the country and the government for conducting a trial with closed doors and before a secret tribunal, and compares the proceedings of this court to the Spanish Inquisition, using the strongest words at his command to intensify the horror which he supposes his announcement will excite throughout the civilized world.

Was this dealing fairly by this government? Was there anything in the conduct of the proceedings here that justified any such remark? Has this been a secret trial? Has it not been conducted in open day in the presence of the accused, and in the presence of seven gentlemen learned in the law, who appeared from day to day as their counsel? Were they not informed of the accusation against them? Were they deprived of the right of challenge? Was it not secured to them by law, and were they not asked to exercise it? Has any part of the evidence been suppressed? Have not all the proceedings been published to the world? What, then, was done, or intended to be done, by the government, which justifies this clamor about a Spanish Inquisition?

That a people assailed by organized treason over an extent of territory half as large as the continent of Europe, and assailed in their very capital by secret assassins banded together and hired to do the work of murder by the instigation of these conspirators, may not be permitted to make inquiry, even with closed doors, touching the nature and extent of the organization, ought not to be asserted by any gentleman who makes the least pretensions to any knowledge of the law, either common, civil, or military. Who does not know that at the common law all inquisition touching crimes and misdemeanors, preparatory to indictment by the grand inquest of the state, is made with closed doors? *Secrecy*

In this trial no parties accused, nor their counsel, nor the reporters of this court, were at any time excluded from its deliberations when any testimony was being taken; nor has there been any testimony taken in the case with closed doors, save that of a few witnesses, who testified, not in regard to the accused or either of them, but in respect to the traitors and conspirators not on trial, who were alleged to have incited this crime. Who is there to say that the American people, in time of armed rebellion and civil war, have not the right to make such an examination as secretly as they may deem necessary, either in a military or civil court?

I have said this, not by way of apology for anything the government has done or attempted to do in the progress of this trial, but to expose the animus of the argument, and to repel the accusation against my country sent out to the world by the counsel. From anything that he has said, I have yet to learn that the American people have not the right to make their inquiries secretly, touching a general conspiracy in aid of an existing rebellion, which involves their nationality and the peace and security of all.

The gentleman then enters into a learned argument for the purpose of showing that, by the Constitution, the people of the United States cannot, in war or in peace, subject any person to trial before a military tribunal, whatever may be his crime or offence, unless such person be in the military or naval service of the United States. The conduct of this argument is as remarkable as its assaults upon the government are unwarranted, and its insinuations about the revival of the Inquisition and secret trials are inexcusable. The court will notice that the argument, from the beginning almost to its conclusion, insists that no person is liable to be tried by military or martial law before a military tribunal, save those in the land and naval service of the United States. I repeat, the conduct of this argument of the gentleman is remarkable. As an instance, I ask the attention, not only of this court, but of that public whom he has ventured to address in this tone and temper, to the authority of the distinguished Chancellor Kent, whose great name the counsel has endeavored to press into his service in support of his general proposition, that no person save those in the military or naval service of the United States is liable to be tried for any crime whatever, either in peace or in war, before a military tribunal.

The language of the gentleman, after citing the provision of the Constitution, "that no person shall be held to answer for a capital or otherwise infamous crime unless on a presentment or indictment of a grand jury, except in cases arising in the land or naval forces, or in the militia, when in actual service in time of war or public danger," is, "that this exception is designed to leave in force, not to enlarge, the power vested in Congress by the original Constitution to make rules for the government and regulation of the land and naval forces; that the land or naval forces are the terms used in both, have the same meaning, and until lately have been supposed by every commentator and judge to exclude from military jurisdiction offences committed by citizens not belonging to such forces." The learned gentleman then adds: "Kent, in a note to his 1st Commentaries, 341, states, and with accuracy, that 'military and naval crimes and offences, committed while the party is attached to and under the immediate authority of the army and navy of the United States and in actual service, are not cognizable under the common-law jurisdiction of the courts of the United States.'" I ask this court to bear in mind that this is the only passage which he quotes from this note of Kent in his argument, and that no man possessed of common sense, however destitute he may be of the exact and varied learning in the law to which the gentleman may rightfully lay claim, can for a moment entertain the opinion that the distinguished chancellor of New York, in the passage just cited, intimates any such thing as the counsel asserts, that the Constitution excludes from military jurisdiction offences committed by citizens not belonging to the land or naval forces.

Who can fail to see that Chancellor Kent, by the passage cited, only decides that military and naval crimes and offences committed by a party attached to and under the immediate authority of the army and navy of the United States, and in actual service, are not cognizable under the common-law jurisdiction of the courts of the United States? He only says they are not cognizable under its common-law jurisdiction; but by that he does not say or intimate, what is attempted to be said by the counsel for him, that "all crimes committed by citizens are by the Constitution excluded from military jurisdiction," and that the perpetrators of them can under no circumstances be tried before military tribunals. Yet the counsel ventures to proceed, standing upon this passage quoted from Kent, to say that, "according to *this* great authority, every other class of persons and every other species of offences are within the jurisdiction of the civil courts, and entitled to the protection of the proceeding by presentment or indictment and the public trial in such a court."

Whatever that great authority may have said elsewhere, it is very doubtful whether any candid man in America will be able to come to the very learned and astute conclusion that Chancellor Kent has so stated in the note or any part of the note which the gentleman has just cited. If he has said it elsewhere, it is for the gentleman, if he relies upon Kent for authority, to produce the passage. But was it fair treatment of this "great authority"—was it not taking an unwarrantable privilege with the distinguished chancellor and his great work, the enduring monument of his learning and genius, to so mutilate the note referred to, as might leave the gentleman at liberty to make his deductions and assertions under cover of the great name of the New York chancellor, to suit the emergency of his case, by omitting the following passage, which occurs in the same note, and absolutely excludes the conclusion so defiantly put forth by the counsel to support his argument? In that note Chancellor Kent says:

"*Military* law is a system of regulations for the government of the armies in the service of the United States, authorized by the act of Congress of April 10, 1806, known as the Articles of War, and *naval* law is a similar system for the government of the navy, under the act of Congress of April 23, 1800. But *martial* law is quite a distinct thing, and is founded upon paramount necessity, and proclaimed by a *military chief.*"

However unsuccessful, after this exposure, the gentleman appears in maintaining his monstrous proposition, that the American people are by their own Constitution forbidden to try the aiders and abettors of armed traitors and rebellion before military tribunals, and subject them, according to the laws of war and the usages of nations, to just punishment for their great crimes, it has been made clear from what I have already stated that he has been eminently successful in mutilating this beautiful production of that great mind; which act of mutilation every one knows is violative alike of the laws of peace and war. Even in war the divine creations of art and the immortal productions of genius and learning are spared.

In the same spirit, and it seems to me with the same unfairness as that just noted, the learned gentleman has very adroitly pressed into his service, by an extract from the autobiography of the war-worn veteran and hero, General Scott, the names of the late Secretary of War, Mr. Marcy, and the learned ex-Attorney General, Mr. Cushing. This adroit performance is achieved in this way: after stating the fact that General Scott in Mexico proclaimed martial law for the trial and punishment by military tribunals of persons guilty of "assassination, murder, and poisoning," the gentleman proceeds to quote from the Autobiography, "that this order, when handed to the then Secretary of War (Mr. Marcy) for his approval, 'a startle at the title (martial law order) was the only comment he then or ever made on the subject,' and that it was 'soon silently returned as too explosive for safe handling.' 'A little later (he adds) the Attorney General (Mr. Cushing) called and asked for a copy, and the law officer of the government, whose business it is to speak on all such matters, was stricken with *legal dumbness.*'" Thereupon the learned gentleman proceeds to say: "How much more startled and more paralyzed would these great men have been had they been consulted on such a commission as this! A commission, not to sit in another country, and to try offences not provided for in any law of the United States, civil or military, then in force, but in their own country, and in a part of it where there are laws providing for their trial and punishment, and civil courts clothed with ample powers for both, and in the daily and undisturbed exercise of their jurisdiction."

I think I may safely say, without stopping to make any special references, that the official career of the late Secretary of War (Mr. Marcy) gave no indication that he ever doubted or denied the constitutional power of the American people, acting through their duly constituted agents, to do any act justified by the laws of war, for the suppression of a rebellion or to repel invasion. Certainly there is nothing in this extract from the Autobiography which justifies any such conclusion. He was startled, we are told. It may have been as much the admiration he had for the boldness and wisdom of the conqueror of Mexico as any abhorrence he had for the trial and punishment of "assassins, poisoners, and murderers," according to the laws and usages of war.

But the official utterances of the ex-Attorney General, Cushing, with which the gentleman doubtless was familiar when he prepared this argument, by no means justify the attempt here made to quote him as authority against the proclamation and enforcement of martial law in time of rebellion and civil war. That distinguished man, not second in legal attainments to any who have held that position, has left an official opinion of record touching this subject. Referring to what is said by Sir Mathew Hale, in his History of the Common Law, concerning martial law, wherein he limits it, as the gentleman has seemed by the whole drift of his argument desirous of doing, and says that it is "not in truth and in reality law, but something indulged rather than allowed as a law—the necessity of government, order, and discipline in an army," Mr. Cushing makes this just criticism : "This proposition is a mere composite blunder, a total misapprehension of the matter. It confounds *martial law* and *law military;* it ascribes to the former the uses of the latter ; it erroneously assumes that the government of a body of troops is a necessity more than of a body of civilians or citizens. It confounds and confuses all the relations of the subject, and is an apt illustration of the incompleteness of the notions of the common-law jurists of England in regard to matters not comprehended in that limited branch of legal science. * * *. Military law, it is now perfectly understood in England, is a branch of the law of the land, applicable only to certain acts of a particular class of persons and administered by special tribunals ; but neither in that nor in any other respect essentially differing as to foundation in constitutional reason from admiralty, ecclesiastical, or indeed chancery and common law. * * * It is the system of rules for the government of the army and navy established by successive acts of Parliament. * * * * Martial law, as exercised in any country by the commander of a foreign army, is an element of the *jus belli*.

" It is incidental to the state of solemn war, and appertains to the law of nations. * * Thus, while the armies of the United States occupied different provinces of the Mexican republic, the respective commanders were not limited in authority by any local law. They allowed, or rather required, the magistrates of the country, municipal or judicial, to continue to administer the laws of the country among their countrymen ; but in subjection, always, to the military power, which acted summarily and according to discretion, when the belligerent interests of the conqueror required it, and which exercised jurisdiction, either summarily or by means of military commissions for the protection or the punishment of citizens of the United States in Mexico."—*Opinions of Attorneys General*, vol. viii, 366–369.

Mr. Cushing says, "That, it would seem, was one of the forms of martial law ;" but he adds, that such an example of martial law administered by a foreign army in the enemy's country "does not enlighten us in regard to the question of martial law in one's own country, and as administered by its military commanders. That is a case which the law of nations does not reach. Its regulation is of the domestic resort of the organic laws of the country itself, and regarding which, as it happens, there is no definite or explicit legislation in the United States, as there is none in England.

"Accordingly, in England, as we have seen, Earl Grey assumes that when martial law exists it has no legal origin, but is a mere fact of necessity, to be legalized afterwards by a bill of indemnity, if there be occasion. I am not prepared to say that, under existing laws, such may not also be the case in the United States."—*Ibid.*, 370.

After such a statement, wherein ex-Attorney General Cushing very clearly recognizes the right of this government, as also of England, to employ martial law as a means of defence in a time of war, whether domestic or foreign, he will be as much surprised when he reads the argument of the learned gentleman, wherein he is described as being struck with *legal dumbness* at the mere mention of proclaiming martial law, and its enforcement by the commander of our army in Mexico, as the late Secretary of War was startled with even the mention of its title.

Even some of the reasons given, and certainly the power exercised by the veteran hero himself, would seem to be in direct conflict with the propositions of the learned gentleman.

The Lieutenant General says, he "excludes from his order cases already cognizable by court-martial, and limits it to cases not provided for in the act of Congress establishing rules and articles for the government of the armies of the United States." Has not the gentleman who attempts to press General Scott into his service argued and insisted upon it, that the commander of the army cannot subject the soldiers under his command to any control or punishment whatever, save that which is provided for in the articles?

It will not do, in order to sustain the gentleman's hypothesis, to say that these provisions of the Constitution, by which he attempts to fetter the power of the people to punish such offences in time of war within the territory of the United States, may be disregarded by an officer of the United States in command of its armies, in the trial and punishment of its soldiers in a foreign war. The law of the United States for the government of its own armies follows the flag upon every sea and in every land.

The truth is, that the right of the people to proclaim and execute martial law is a necessary incident of war, and this was the right exercised, and rightfully exercised, by Lieutenant General Scott in Mexico. It was what Earl Grey has justly said was a "fact of necessity," and I may add, an act as clearly authorized as was the act of fighting the enemy when they appeared before him.

In making this exception, the Lieutenant General followed the rule recognized by the American authorities on military law, in which it is declared that "many crimes committed even by military officers, enlisted men, or camp retainers, cannot be tried under the rules and articles of war. Military commissions must be resorted to for such cases, and these commissions should be ordered by the same authority, be constituted in a similar manner, and their proceedings be conducted according to the same general rules as general courts-martial."—*Benet*, 15.

There remain for me to notice, at present, two other points in this extraordinary speech: first, that martial law does not warrant a military commission for the trial of military offences—that is, offences committed in time of war in the interests of the public enemy, and by concert and agreement with the enemy; and second, that martial law does not prevail in the United States, and has never been declared by any competent authority.

It is not necessary, as the gentleman himself has declined to argue the first point,—whether martial law authorizes the organization of military commissions by order of the Commander-in-Chief to try such offences, that I should say more than that the authority just cited by me shows that such commissions are authorized under martial law, and are created by the commander for the trial of all such offences, when their punishment by court-martial is not provided for by the express statute law of the country.

The second point,—that martial law has not been declared by any competent authority, is an arraignment of the late murdered President of the United States for his proclamation of September 24, 1862, declaring martial law throughout the United States; and of which, in Lawrence's edition of Wheaton on International Law, p. 522, it is said, "Whatever may be the inference to be deduced either from constitutional or international law, or from the usages of European governments, as to the legitimate depository of the power of suspending the writ of *habeas corpus*, the virtual abrogation of the judiciary in cases affecting individual liberty, and the establishment as *matter of fact* in the United States, by the Executive alone, of martial law, not merely in the insurrectionary districts, or in cases of military occupancy, but throughout the entire Union, and not temporarily, but as an institution as permanent as the insurrection on which it professes to be based, and capable on the same principle of being revived in all cases of foreign as well as civil war, are placed beyond question by the President's proclamation of September 24, 1862." That proclamation is as follows:

"BY THE PRESIDENT OF THE UNITED STATES OF AMERICA.

"A PROCLAMATION.

"Whereas it has become necessary to call into service not only volunteers, but also portions of the militia of the States, by a draft, in order to suppress the insurrection existing in the United States, and disloyal persons are not adequately restrained by the ordinary processes of law from hindering this measure, and from giving aid and comfort in various ways to the insurrection: Now, therefore, be it ordered, that during the existing insurrection, and as a necessary means for suppressing the same, all rebels and insurgents, their aiders and abettors, within the United States, and all persons discouraging volunteer enlistments, resisting militia drafts, or guilty of any disloyal practice, affording aid and comfort to rebels, against the authority of the United States, shall be subject to martial law, and liable to trial and punishment by courts-martial or military commission.

"Second. That the writ of *habeas corpus* is suspended in respect to all persons arrested, or who are now, or hereafter during the rebellion shall be, imprisoned in any fort, camp, arsenal, military prison, or other place of confinement, by any military authority, or by the sentence of any court martial or military commission.

"In witness whereof, I have hereunto set my hand, and caused the seal of the United States to be affixed.

"Done at the city of Washington, this 24th day of September, A. D. 1862, and of the independence of the United States the eighty-seventh.

"ABRAHAM LINCOLN.

"By the President:
"WILLIAM H. SEWARD,
"*Secretary of State.*"

This proclamation is duly certified from the War Department to be in full force and not revoked, and is evidence of record in this case; and but a few days since a proclamation of the President, of which this court will take notice, declares that the same remains in full force.

It has been said by another of the counsel for the accused (Mr. Stone) in his argument, that, admitting its validity, the proclamation ceases to have effect with the insurrection, and is terminated by it. It is true the proclamation of martial law only continues during the insurrection; but inasmuch as the question of the existence of an insurrection is a political question, the decision of which belongs exclusively to the political department of the government, that department alone can declare its existence, and that department alone can declare its termination, and by the action of the political department of the government every judicial tribunal in the land is concluded and bound. That question has been settled for fifty years in this country by the Supreme Court of the United States : First, in the case of Brown vs. The United States (8 Cranch;) also in the prize cases (2 Black, 641.) Nothing more, therefore, need be said upon this question of an *existing* insurrection than this: The political department of the government has heretofore proclaimed an insurrection, that department has not yet declared the insurrection ended, and the event on the 14th of April, which robbed the people of their chosen Executive, and clothed this land in mourning, bore sad but overwhelming witness to the fact that the rebellion is not ended. The fact of the insurrection is not an open question to be tried or settled by parol, either in a military tribunal or in a civil court.

The declaration of the learned gentleman who opened the defence, (Mr. Johnson,) that martial law has never been declared by any competent authority, as I have already said, arraigns Mr. Lincoln for a usurpation of power. Does the gentleman mean to say that, until Congress authorizes it, the President cannot proclaim and enforce martial law in the suppression of armed and organized rebellion ? Or does he only affirm that this act of the late President is a usurpation ?

The proclamation of martial law in 1862 a usurpation ! though it armed the people in that dark hour of trial with the means of defence against traitorous and secret enemies in every State and district of the country; though by its use some of the guilty were brought to swift and just judgment, and others deterred from crime or driven to flight; though by this means the innocent and defenceless were protected; though by this means the city of the gentleman's residence was saved from the violence and pillage of the mob and the torch of the incendiary. But, says the gentleman, it was a usurpation, forbidden by the laws of the land !

The same was said of the proclamations of blockade issued April 19 and 27, 1861, which declared a blockade of the ports of the insurgent States, and that all vessels violating the same were subjects of capture, and, together with the cargo, to be condemned as prize. Inasmuch as Congress had not then recognized the fact of civil war, these proclamations were denounced as void. The Supreme Court decided otherwise, and affirmed the power of the Executive thus to subject property on the seas to seizure and condemnation. I read from that decision:

"The Constitution confers upon the President the whole executive power; he is bound to take care that the laws be faithfully executed; he is commander-in-chief of the army and navy of the United States, and of the militia of the several States when called into the actual service of the United States. * * Whether the President, in fulfilling his duties as commander-in-chief in suppressing an insurrection, has met with such armed hostile resistance, and a civil war of such alarming proportions as will compel him to accord to them the character of belligerents, is a question to be decided *by him*, and this court must be governed by the decisions and acts of the political department of the government to which this power was intrusted. He must determine what degree of force the crisis demands.

"The proclamation of blockade is itself official and conclusive evidence to the court that a state of war existed which demanded and authorized a recourse to such a measure under the circumstances peculiar to the case." (2 Black, 670.)

It has been solemnly ruled by the same tribunal, in an earlier case, " that the power is confided to the Executive of the Union to determine when it is necessary to call out the militia of the States to repel invasion," as follows: "That he is necessarily constituted the judge of the existence of the exigency in the first instance, and is bound to act according to his belief of the facts. If he does so act, and decides to call forth the militia, his orders for this purpose are in strict conformity with the provisions of the law ; and it would seem to follow as a necessary consequence, that every act done by a subordinate officer, in obedience to such orders, is equally justifiable. The law contemplates that, under such circumstances, orders shall be given to carry the power into effect ; and it cannot therefore be a correct inference that any other person has a just right to disobey them. The law does not provide for any appeal from the judgment of the President, or for any right in subordinate officers to review his decision, and in effect defeat it. Whenever a statute gives a discretionary power to any person, to be exercised by him upon his own opinion of certain facts, it is a sound rule of construction, that the statute constitutes him the sole and exclusive judge of the existence of those facts." (12 Wheaton, 31.)

In the light of these decisions, it must be clear to every mind that the question of the existence of an insurrection, and the necessity of calling into requisition for its suppression both the militia of the

States and the army and navy of the United States, and of proclaiming martial law, which is an essential condition of war, whether foreign or domestic, must rest with the officer of the government who is charged by the express terms of the Constitution with the performance of this great duty for the common defence and the execution of the laws of the Union.

But it is further insisted by the gentleman in this argument, that Congress has not authorized the establishment of military commissions, which are essential to the judicial administration of martial law and the punishment of crimes committed during the existence of a civil war, and especially, that such commissions are not so authorized to try persons other than those in the military or naval service of the United States, or in the militia of the several States, when in the actual service of the United States. The gentleman's argument assuredly destroys itself, for ho insists that the Congress, as the legislative department of the government, can pass no law which, either in peace or war, can constitutionally subject any citizen not in the land or naval forces to trial for crime before a military tribunal, or otherwise than by a jury in the civil courts.

Why does the learned gentleman now tell us that Congress has not authorized this to be done, after declaring just as stoutly that by the fifth and sixth amendments to the Constitution no such military tribunals can be established for the trial of any person not in the military or naval service of the United States, or in the militia when in actual service, for the commission of any crime whatever in time of war or insurrection? It ought to have occurred to the gentleman when commenting upon the exception in the fifth article of the Constitution, that there was a reason for it very different from that which he saw fit to assign, and that reason, manifestly upon the face of the Constitution itself, was, that by the eighth section of the first article, it is expressly provided, that Congress shall have power to make rules for the government of the land and naval forces, and to provide for organizing, arming, and disciplining the militia, and for *governing* such part of them as may be employed in the service of the United States, and that, inasmuch as military discipline and order are as essential in an army in time of peace, as in time of war, if the Constitution would leave this power to Congress in peace, it must make the exception, so that rules and regulations for the government of the army and navy should be operative in time of peace as well as in time of war; because the provisions of the Constitution give the right of trial by jury IN TIME OF PEACE, in all criminal prosecutions by indictment, in terms embracing every human being that may be held to answer for crime in the United States : and therefore if the eighth section of the first article was to remain in full force IN TIME OF PEACE, the exception must be made ; and accordingly, the exception was made. But by the argument we have listened to, this court is told, and the country is told, that IN TIME OF WAR—a war which involves in its dread issue the lives and interests of us all—the guarantees of the Constitution are in full force for the benefit of those who conspire with the enemy, creep into your camps, murder in cold blood, in the interests of the invader or insurgent, the commander-in-chief of your army, and secure to him the slow and weak provisions of the civil law, while the soldier, who may, when overcome by the demands of exhausted nature, which cannot be resisted, have slept at his post, is subject to be tried upon the spot by a military tribunal and shot. The argument amounts to this: that as military courts and military trials of civilians in time of war are a usurpation and tyranny, and as soldiers are liable to such arrests and trial, Sergeant Corbett, who shot Booth, should be tried and executed by sentence of a military court; while Booth's co-conspirators and aiders should be saved from any such indignity as a military trial ! I confess that I am too dull to comprehend the logic, the reason, or the sense of such a conclusion ! If there is any one *entitled* to this privilege of a civil trial, at a remote period, and by a jury of the District, IN TIME OF CIVIL WAR, when the foundations of the republic are rocking beneath the earthquake tread of armed rebellion, that man is the defender of the republic. It will never do to say, as has been said in this argument, that the soldier is not liable to be tried in time of war by a military tribunal for any other offence than those prescribed in the rules and articles of war. To my mind, nothing can be clearer than that citizen and soldier alike, in time of civil or foreign war, after a proclamation of martial law, are triable by military tribunals for all offences of which they may be guilty, in the interests of, or in concert with, the enemy.

These provisions, therefore, of your Constitution for indictment and trial by jury in civil courts of *all crimes* are, as I shall hereafter show, silent and inoperative in time of war when the public safety requires it.

The argument to which I have thus been replying, as the court will not fail to perceive, nor that public to which the argument is addressed, is a labored attempt to establish the proposition, that, by the Constitution of the United States, the American people cannot, even in a civil war the greatest the world has ever seen, employ martial law and military tribunals as a means of successfully asserting their authority, preserving their nationality, and securing protection to the lives and property of all, and especially to the persons of those to whom they have committed, officially, the great trust of maintaining the national authority. The gentleman says, with an air of perfect confidence, that he denies the jurisdiction of military tribunals for the trial of civilians in time of war, because neither the Constitution nor laws justify, but on the contrary repudiate them, and that all the experience of the past is against it. I might content myself with saying that the practice of all nations is against the gentleman's conclusion. The struggle for our national independence was aided and prosecuted by military tribunals and martial law, as well as by arms. The contest for American nationality began with the establishment, very soon after the firing of the first gun at Lexington on the 19th day of April, 1775, of military tribunals and martial law. On the 30th of June, 1775, the Continental Congress provided that "whosoever, *belonging to the continental army*, shall be convicted of holding correspondence with, or giving intelligence to the enemy, either indirectly or directly, shall suffer such punishment as by a court-martial shall be ordered." This was found not sufficient, inasmuch as it did not reach those *civilians* who, like certain civilians of our day, claim the protection of the civil law in time of war against military arrests and military trials for military crimes. Therefore, the same Congress, on the 7th of November, 1775, amended this provision by striking out the words "belonging to the continental army," and adopting the article as follows:

"*All persons* convicted of holding a treacherous correspondence with, or giving intelligence to the enemy, shall suffer death or such other punishment as a general court-martial shall think proper."

And on the 17th of June, 1776, the Congress added an additional rule—

"That all persons, not members of, nor owing allegiance to, any of the United States of America, who should be found lurking as spies in or about the fortifications or encampments of the armies of the United States, or any of them, shall suffer death, according to the law and usage of nations, by the sentence of a court-martial, or such other punishment as a court-martial shall direct."

Comprehensive as was this legislation, embracing as it did soldiers, citizens, and aliens, subjecting all alike to trial for their military crimes by the military tribunals of justice, according to the law and the usage of nations, it was found to be insufficient to meet that most dangerous of all crimes committed in the interests of the enemy by citizens in time of war—the crime of conspiring together to assassinate or seize and carry away the soldiers and citizens who were loyal to the cause of the country. Therefore, on the 27th of February, 1778, the Congress adopted the following resolution:

"*Resolved*, That whatever inhabitant of these States shall kill, or seize, or take any loyal citizen or citizens thereof and convey him, her, or them to any place within the power of the enemy, or shall ENTER INTO ANY COMBINATION for such purpose, or attempt to carry the same into execution, or hath assisted or shall assist therein; or shall, by giving intelligence, acting as a guide, or in any manner whatever, aid the enemy in the perpetration thereof, he shall suffer death by the judgment of a court-martial as a traitor, assassin, or spy, if the offence be committed within seventy miles of the headquarters of the grand or other armies of these States where a general officer commands."—*Journals of Congress*, vol. ii, pp. 459, 460.

So stood the law until the adoption of the Constitution of the United States. Every well-informed man knows that at the time of the passage of these acts, the courts of justice having cognizance of all crimes against persons, were open in many of the States, and that by their several constitutions and charters, which were then the supreme law for the punishment of crimes committed within their respective territorial limits, no man was liable to conviction but by the verdict of a jury. Take, for example, the provisions of the constitution of North Carolina, adopted on the 10th of November, 1776, and in full force at the time of the passage of the last resolution by Congress above cited, which provisions are as follows:

"That no freeman shall be put to answer any criminal charge but by indictment, presentment, or impeachment."

"That no freeman shall be convicted of any crime but by the unanimous verdict of a jury of good and lawful men in open court, as heretofore used."

This was the law in 1778 in all the States, and the provision for a trial by jury every one knows meant a jury of twelve men, impannelled and qualified to try the issue in a civil court. The conclusion is not to be avoided, that these enactments of the Congress under the Confederation set aside the trial by jury within the several States, and expressly provided for the trial by court-martial of "any of the inhabitants" who, during the revolution, might, contrary to the provisions of said law, and in aid of the public enemy, give them intelligence, or kill any loyal citizens of the United States, or enter into any combination to kill or carry them away. How comes it, if the argument of the counsel be true, that this enactment was passed by the Congress of 1778, when the constitutions of the several

States at that day as fully guaranteed trial by jury to every person held to answer for a crime, as does the Constitution of the United States at this hour? Notwithstanding this fact, I have yet to learn that any loyal man ever challenged, during all the period of our conflict for independence and nationality, the validity of that law for the trial, for military offences, by military tribunals, of all offenders, as the law, not of peace, but of war, and absolutely essential to the prosecution of war. I may be pardoned for saying that it is the accepted common law of nations, that martial-law is, at all times and everywhere, essential to the successful prosecution of war, whether it be a civil or a foreign war. The validity of these acts of the Continental and Confederate Congress I know was challenged, but only by men charged with the guilt of their country's blood.

Washington, the peerless, the stainless, and the just, with whom God walked through the night of that great trial, enforced this just and wise enactment upon all occasions. On the 30th of September, 1780, Joshua H. Smith, by the order of General Washington, was put upon his trial before a court-martial, convened in the State of New York, on the charge of there aiding and assisting Benedict Arnold, in a combination with the enemy, to *take, kill,* and *seize* such loyal citizens or soldiers of the United States as were in garrison at West Point. Smith objected to the jurisdiction, averring that he was a private citizen, not in the military or naval service, and therefore was only amenable to the civil authority of the State, whose constitution had guaranteed the right of trial by jury to all persons held to answer for crime. (Chandler's Criminal Trials, vol. 2, p. 187.) The constitution of New York then in force had so provided; but, notwithstanding that, the court overruled the plea, held him to answer, and tried him. I repeat, that when Smith was thus tried by court-martial, the constitution of New York as fully guaranteed trial by jury in the civil courts to all civilians charged and held to answer for crimes within the limits of that State, as does the Constitution of the United States guarantee such trial within the limits of the District of Columbia. By the second of the Articles of Confederation each State retained "its sovereignty," and every power, jurisdiction, and right not *expressly* delegated to the United States in Congress assembled. By those articles there was no express delegation of judicial power; therefore the States retained it fully.

If the military courts, constituted by the commander of the army of the United States under the Confederation, who was appointed only by a resolution of the Congress, without any *express* grant of power to authorize it—his office not being created by the act of the people in their fundamental law—had jurisdiction in every State to try and put to death "any inhabitant" thereof who should *kill* any loyal citizen or enter into "any combination" for any such purpose therein in time of war, notwithstanding the provisions of the constitution and laws of such States, how can any man conceive that under the Constitution of the United States, which is the supreme law over every State, anything in the constitution and laws of such State to the contrary notwithstanding, and the supreme law over every Territory of the republic as well, the Commander-in-Chief of the army of the United States, who is made such by the Constitution, and by its supreme authority clothed with the power and charged with the duty of directing and controlling the whole military power of the United States in time of rebellion or invasion, has not that authority?

I need not remind the court that one of the marked differences between the Articles of Confederation and the Constitution of the United States was, that, under the Confederation, the Congress was the sole depository of all federal power. The Congress of the Confederation, said Madison, held "the command of the army." (Fed., No. 38.) Has the Constitution, which was ordained by the people the better "to insure domestic tranquillity and to provide for the common defence," so fettered the great power of self-defence against armed insurrection or invasion that martial law, so essential in war, is forbidden by that great instrument? I will yield to no man in reverence for or obedience to the Constitution of my country, esteeming it, as I do, a new evangel to the nations, embodying the democracy of the New Testament—the absolute equality of all men before the law, in respect of those rights of human nature which are the gift of God, and therefore as universal as the material structure of man. Can it be that this Constitution of ours, so divine in its spirit of justice, so beneficent in its results, so full of wisdom and goodness and truth, under which we became one people, a great and powerful nationality, has, in terms or by implication, denied to this people the power to crush armed rebellion by war, and to arrest and punish, during the existence of such rebellion, according to the laws of war and the usages of nations, secret conspirators, who aid and abet the public enemy?

Here is a conspiracy, organized and prosecuted by armed traitors and hired assassins, receiving the moral support of thousands in every State and district, who pronounced the war for the Union a failure, and your now murdered but immortal Commander-in-Chief a tyrant; the object of which conspiracy, as the testimony shows, was to aid the tottering rebellion which struck at the nation's life. It is in evidence that Davis, Thompson, and others, chiefs in this rebellion, in aid of the same, agreed and conspired with others to poison the fountains of water which supply your commercial metropolis, and thereby murder its inhabitants; to secretly deposit in the habitations of the people and in the ships in your harbors inflammable materials, and thereby destroy them by fire; to murder by the slow and consuming torture of famine your soldiers, captive in their hands; to import pestilence in infected clothes to be distributed in your capital and camps, and thereby murder the surviving heroes and defenders of the republic, who, standing by the holy graves of your unreturning brave, proudly and defiantly challenge to honorable combat and open battle all public enemies, that their country may live; and, finally, to crown this horrid catalogue of crime, this sum of all human atrocities, conspired, as charged upon your record, with the accused and John Wilkes Booth and John H. Surratt, to kill and murder in your capital the executive officers of your government and the commander of your armies. When this conspiracy, entered into by these traitors, is revealed by its attempted execution, and the foul and brutal murder of your President in the capital, you are told that it is unconstitutional, in order to arrest the further execution of the conspiracy, to interpose the military power of this government for the arrest, without civil process, of any of the parties thereto, and for their trial by a military tribunal of justice. If any such rule had obtained during our struggle for independence, we never would have been a nation. If any such rule had been adopted and acted upon now, during the fierce struggle of the past four years, no man can say that our nationality would have thus long survived.

The whole people of the United States by their Constitution have created the office of President of the United States and commander-in-chief of the army and navy, and have vested, by the terms of that Constitution, in the person of the President and commander-in-chief, the power to enforce the execution of the laws, and preserve, protect, and defend the Constitution.

The question may well be asked : If, as commander-in-chief, the President may not, in time of insurrection or war, proclaim and execute martial law, according to the usages of nations, how he can successfully perform the duties of his office—execute the laws, preserve the Constitution, suppress insurrection, and repel invasion ?

Martial law and military tribunals are as essential to the successful prosecution of war as are men, and arms, and munitions. The Constitution of the United States has vested the power to declare war and raise armies and navies exclusively in the Congress, and the power to prosecute the war and command the army and navy exclusively in the President of the United States. As, under the Confederation, the commander of the army, appointed only by the Congress, was by the resolution of that Congress empowered to act as he might think proper for the good and welfare of the service, subject only to such restraints or orders as the Congress might give; so, under the Constitution, the President is, by the people who ordained that Constitution and declared him commander-in-chief of the army and navy, vested with full power to direct and control the army and navy of the United States, and employ all the forces necessary to preserve, protect, and defend the Constitution and execute the laws, as enjoined by his oath and the very letter of the Constitution, subject to no restriction or direction save such as Congress may from time to time prescribe.

That these powers for the common defence, intrusted by the Constitution exclusively to the Congress and the President, are, in time of civil war or foreign invasion, to be exercised without limitation or restraint, to the extent of the public necessity, and without any intervention of the federal judiciary or of State constitutions or State laws, are facts in our history not open to question.

The position is not to be answered by saying you make the American Congress thereby omnipotent, and clothe the American Executive with the asserted attribute of hereditary monarchy—the king can do no wrong. Let the position be fairly stated—that the Congress and President, in war as in peace, are but the agents of the whole people, and that this unlimited power for the common defence against armed rebellion or foreign invasion is but the power of the people intrusted exclusively to the legislative and executive departments as their agents, for any and every abuse of which these agents are directly responsible to the people—and the demagogue cry of an omnipotent Congress, and an Executive invested with royal prerogatives, vanishes like the baseless fabric of a vision. If the Congress, corruptly, or oppressively, or wantonly abuse this great trust, the people by the irresistible power of the ballot hurl them from place. If the President so abuse the trust, the people by their Congress withhold supplies, or by impeachment transfer the trust to better hands, strip him of the franchises of citizenship and of office, and declare him forever disqualified to hold any position of honor, trust, or power under the government of his country.

I can understand very well why men should tremble at the exercise of this great power by a monarch whose person, by the constitution of his realm, is inviolable, but I cannot conceive how any American citizen, who has faith in the capacity of the whole people to govern themselves, should give himself any concern on the subject. Mr. Hallam, the distinguished author of the Constitutional History of England, has said:

"Kings love to display the divinity with which their flatterers invest them in nothing so much as in the instantaneous execution of their will, and to stand revealed, as it were, in the storm and thunderbolt when their power breaks through the operation of secondary causes and awes a prostrate nation without the intervention of law."

How just are such words when applied to an irresponsible monarch! how absurd, when applied to a whole people, acting through their duly appointed agents, whose will, thus declared, is the supreme law, to awe into submission and peace and obedience, not a prostrate nation, but a prostrate rebellion! The same great author utters the fact which all history attests, when he says:

"It has been usual for all governments during actual rebellion to proclaim martial law for the suspension of civil jurisdiction; and this anomaly, I must admit," he adds, "is very far from being less indispensable at such unhappy seasons where the ordinary mode of trial is by jury, than where the right of decision resides in the court."—*Const. Hist.*, vol. i, ch. 5, p. 326.

That the power to proclaim martial law and fully or partially suspend the civil jurisdiction, federal and state, in time of rebellion or civil war, and punish by military tribunals all offences committed in aid of the public enemy, is conferred upon Congress and the Executive, necessarily results from the unlimited grants of power for the common defence to which I have already briefly referred. I may be pardoned for saying that this position is not assumed by me for the purposes of this occasion, but that early in the first year of this great struggle for our national life I proclaimed it as a representative of the people, under the obligation of my oath, and, as I then believed, and still believe, upon the authority of the great men who formed and fashioned the wise and majestic fabric of American government.

Some of the citations which I deemed it my duty at that time to make, and some of which I now reproduce, have, I am pleased to say, found a wider circulation in books that have since been published by others.

When the Constitution was on trial for its deliverance before the people of the several States, its ratification was opposed on the ground that it conferred upon Congress and the Executive unlimited power for the common defence. To all such objectors—and they were numerous in every State—that great man, Alexander Hamilton, whose words will live as long as our language lives, speaking to the listening people of all the States and urging them not to reject that matchless instrument which bore the name of Washington, said :

"The authorities essential to the care of the common defence are these: To raise armies ; to build and equip fleets; to prescribe rules for the government of both ; to direct their operations ; to provide for their support. These powers ought to exist WITHOUT LIMITATION ; because it is impossible to foresee or define the extent and variety of national exigencies, and the correspondent extent and variety of the means which may be necessary to satisfy them.

"The circumstances that endanger the safety of nations are infinite ; and for this reason no constitutional shackles can wisely be imposed on the power to which the care of it is committed. * * * This power ought to be under the direction of the same councils which are appointed to preside over the common defence. * * * It must be admitted, as a necessary consequence, that there can be no limitation of that authority which is to provide for the defence and protection of the community, in any manner essential to its efficacy; that is, in any matter essential to the formation, direction, or support of the national forces."

He adds the further remark : " This is one of those truths which, to a correct and unprejudiced mind, carries its own evidence along with it; and may be obscured, but cannot be made plainer by argument or reasoning. It rests upon axioms as simple as they are universal—the *means* ought to be proportioned to the *end;* the persons from whose agency the attainment of any *end* is expected ought to possess the means by which it is to be attained."—*Federalist*, No. 23.

In the same great contest for the adoption of the Constitution Madison, sometimes called the Father of the Constitution, said:

" Is the power of declaring war necessary ? No man will answer this question in the negative. * * * Is the power of raising armies and equipping fleets necessary ? * * * It is involved in the power of self-defence. * * * With what color of propriety could the force necessary for defence be limited by those who cannot limit the force of offence ? * * * The means of security can only be regulated by the means and the danger of attack. * * * It is in vain to oppose constitutional barriers to the impulse of self-preservation. It is worse than in vain, because it plants in the Constitution itself necessary usurpations of power."—*Federalist*, No. 41.

With this construction, proclaimed both by the advocates and opponents of its ratification, the Constitution of the United States was accepted and adopted, and that construction has been followed and acted upon, by every department of the government to this day.

It was as well understood then in theory as it has since been illustrated in practice, that the judicial power, both federal and State, had no voice and could exercise no authority in the conduct and prosecution of a war, except in subordination to the political department of the government. The Constitution contains the significant provision, "The privilege of the writ of habeas corpus shall not be suspended, unless when in cases of rebellion or invasion the public safety may require it."

What was this but a declaration, that in time of rebellion, or invasion, the public safety is the highest law?—that so far as necessary the civil courts (of which the Commander-in-Chief, under the direction of Congress, shall be the sole judge) must be silent, and the rights of each citizen, as secured in time of peace, must yield to the wants, interests, and necessities of the nation? Yet we have been gravely told by the gentleman, in his argument, that the maxim, *salus populi suprema est lex*, is but fit for a tyrant's use.. Those grand men, whom God taught to build the fabric of empire, thought otherwise, when they put that maxim into the Constitution of their country. It is very clear that the Constitution recognizes the great principle which underlies the structure of society and of all civil government; that no man lives for himself alone, but each for all; that, if need be, some must die, that the State may live, because at best the individual is but for to-day, while the commonwealth is for all time. I agree with the gentleman in the maxim which he borrows from Aristotle, "Let the public weal be under the protection of the law ;" but I claim that in war, as in peace, by the very terms of the Constitution of the country, the public safety is under the protection of the law; that the Constitution itself has provided for the declaration of war for the common defence, to suppress rebellion, to repel invasion, and, by express terms, has declared that whatever is necessary to make the prosecution of the war successful, may be done, and ought to be done, and is therefore constitutionally lawful.

Who will dare to say that in time of civil war "no person shall be deprived of life, liberty, and property, without due process of law ?" This is a provision of your Constitution than which there is none more just or sacred in it; it is, however, only the law of peace, not of war. In peace, that wise provision of the Constitution must be, and is, enforced by the civil courts ; in war, it must be, and is, to a great extent, inoperative and disregarded. The thousands slain by your armies in battle were deprived of life "without due process of law." All spies arrested, convicted, and executed by your military tribunals in time of war are deprived of liberty and life "without due process of law;" all enemies captured and held as prisoners of war are deprived of liberty "without due process of law;" all owners whose property is forcibly seized and appropriated in war are deprived of their property "without due process of law." The Constitution recognizes the principle of common law, that every man's house is his castle; that his home, the shelter of his wife and children, is his most sacred possession; and has therefore specially provided, "that no soldier shall *in time of peace* be quartered in any house, without the consent of its owner, nor in time of war, but in a manner to be prescribed by law, [III Amend.;] thereby declaring that, in time of war, Congress may by law authorize, as it has done, that without the consent and against the consent of the owner, the soldier may be quartered in any man's house, and upon any man's hearth. What I have said illustrates the proposition, that in time of war the civil tribunals of justice are wholly or partially silent, as the public safety may require; that the limitations and provisions of the Constitution in favor of life, liberty and property are therefore wholly or partially suspended. In this I am sustained by an authority second to none with intelligent American citizens. Mr. John Quincy Adams, than whom a purer man or a wiser statesman never ascended the chair of the chief magistracy in America, said in his place in the House of Representatives, in 1836, that:

" In the authority given to Congress by the Constitution of the United States to declare war, all the powers incident to war are by necessary implication conferred upon the government of the United States. Now the powers incidental to war are derived, not from their internal municipal source, but from the laws and usages of nations. There are, then, in the authority of Congress and of the Executive two classes of powers altogether different in their nature and often incompatible with each other, the war power and the peace power. The peace power is limited by regulations and restricted by provisions prescribed within the Constitution itself. The war power is limited only by the laws and usage of nations. This power is tremendous; it is strictly constitutional, but it breaks down every barrier so anxiously erected for the protection of liberty, of property, and of life."

If this be so, how can there be trial by jury for military offences in time of civil war? If you cannot, and do not, try the armed enemy before you shoot him, or the captured enemy before you imprison him, why should you be held to open the civil courts and try the spy, the conspirator, and the assassin, in the secret service of the public enemy, by jury, before you convict and punish him? Why not clamor against holding imprisoned the captured armed rebels, deprived of their liberty without due process of law? Are they not citizens? Why not clamor against slaying for their crime of treason, which is cognizable in the civil courts, by your rifled ordnance and the leaden hail of your musketry in battle, these public enemies, without trial by jury? Are they not citizens? Why is the clamor confined exclusively to the trial by military tribunals of justice of traitorous spies, traitorous conspirators, and assassins hired to do secretly what the armed rebel attempts to do openly—murder your nationality by assassinating its defenders and its executive officers? Nothing can be clearer than that the rebel captured prisoner, being a citizen of the republic, is as much entitled to trial by jury before he is committed to prison, as the spy, or the aider and abettor of the treason by conspiracy and assassination, being a citizen, is entitled to such trial by jury, before he is subjected to the just punishment of the law for his great crime. I think that in time of war the remark of Montesquieu, touching the civil judiciary, is true: that "it is next to nothing." Hamilton well said, "The Executive holds the sword of the community; the judiciary has no direction of the strength of society; it has neither force nor will; it has judgment alone, and is dependent for the execution of that upon the arm of the Executive." The people of these States so understood the Constitution, and adopted it; and intended thereby, without limitation or restraint, to empower their Congress and Executive to authorize by law, and execute by force, whatever the public safety might require, to suppress rebellion or repel invasion.

Notwithstanding all that has been said by the counsel for the accused to the contrary, the Constitution has received this construction from the day of its adoption to this hour. The Supreme Court of the United States has solemnly decided that the Constitution has conferred upon the government authority to employ all the means necessary to the faithful execution of all the powers which that Constitution enjoins upon the government of the United States, and upon every department and every officer thereof. Speaking of that provision of the Constitution which provides that "Congress shall have power to make all laws that may be necessary and proper to carry into effect all powers granted to the government of the United States, or to any department or officer thereof," Chief Justice Marshall, in his great decision in the case of McCulloch *vs.* State of Maryland, says:

"The powers given to the government imply the ordinary means of execution, and the government, in all sound reason and fair interpretation, must have the choice of the means which it deems the most convenient and appropriate to the execution of the power. * * * The powers of the government were given for the welfare of the nation; they were intended to endure for ages to come, and to be adapted to the various crises in human affairs. To prescribe the specific means by which government should, in all future time, execute its power, and to confine the choice of means to such narrow limits as should not leave it in the power of Congress to adopt any which might be appropriate and conducive to the end, would be most unwise and pernicious."—(4 Wheaton, 420.)

Words fitly spoken! which illustrated at the time of their utterance the wisdom of the Constitution in providing this general grant of power to meet every possible exigency which the fortunes of war might cast upon the country, and the wisdom of which words, in turn, has been illustrated to-day by the gigantic and triumphant struggle of the people during the last four years for the supremacy of the Constitution, and in exact accordance with its provisions. In the light of these wonderful events, the words of Pinckney, uttered when the illustrious Chief Justice had concluded this opinion, "The Constitution of my country is immortal!" seem to have become words of prophecy. Has not this great tribunal, through the chief of all its judges, by this luminous and profound reasoning, declared that the government may by law authorize the Executive to employ, in the prosecution of war, the ordinary means, and all the means necessary and adapted to the end? And in the other decision, before referred to, in the 8th of Cranch, arising during the late war with Great Britain, Mr. Justice Story said:

"When the legislative authority, to whom the right to declare war is confided, has declared war in its most unlimited manner, the executive authority, to whom the execution of the war is confided, is bound to carry it into effect. He has a discretion vested in him as to the manner and extent, but he cannot lawfully transcend the rules of warfare established among civilized nations. He cannot lawfully exercise powers or authorize proceedings which the civilized world repudiates and disclaims. The sovereignty, as to declaring war and limiting its effects, rests with the legislature. The sovereignty as to its execution rests with the President."—(Brown *vs.* United States, 8 Cranch, 153.)

Has the Congress, to whom is committed the sovereignty of the whole people to declare war, by legislation restricted the President, or attempted to restrict him, in the prosecution of this war for the Union, from exercising all the "powers" and adopting all the "proceedings" usually approved and employed by the civilized world? He would, in my judgment, be a bold man who asserted that Congress has so legislated; and the Congress which should by law fetter the executive arm when raised for the common defence would, in my opinion, be false to their oath. That Congress may prescribe rules for the government of the army and navy and the militia when in actual service, by articles of war, is an express grant of power in the Constitution, which Congress has rightfully exercised, and which the Executive must and does obey. That Congress may aid the Executive by legislation in the prosecution of a war, civil or foreign, is admitted. That Congress may restrain the Executive, and arraign, try, and condemn him for wantonly abusing the great trust, is expressly declared in the Constitution. That Congress shall pass all laws NECESSARY to enable the Executive to execute the laws of the Union, suppress insurrection, and repel invasion, is one of the express requirements of the Constitution, for the performance of which the Congress is bound by an oath.

What was the legislation of Congress when treason fired its first gun on Sumter? By the act of 1795 it is provided that whenever the laws of the United States shall be opposed, or the execution thereof obstructed, in any State, by combinations too powerful to be suppressed by the ordinary course of judicial proceeding or by the powers vested in the marshals, it shall be lawful by this act for the President to call forth the militia of such State, or of any other State or States, as may be necessary to suppress such combinations and to cause the laws to be executed. (1st Statutes at Large, 424.) By the act of 1807 it is provided that in case of insurrection or obstruction to the laws, either of the United States or of any individual State or Territory, where it is lawful for the President of the United States to call forth the militia for the purpose of suppressing such insurrection or of causing the laws to be duly executed, it shall be lawful for him to employ for such purpose such part of the land or naval forces of the United States as shall be judged necessary. (2d Statutes at Large, 443.)

Can any one doubt that by these acts the President is clothed with full power to determine whether armed insurrection exists in any State or Territory of the Union; and if so, to make war upon it with all the force he may deem necessary or be able to command? By the simple exercise of this great power it necessarily results that he may, in the prosecution of the war for the suppression of such insurrection. suspend as far as may be necessary the civil administration of justice by substituting in its stead martial law, which is simply the common law of war. If in such a moment the President may make no arrests without civil warrant, and may inflict no violence or penalties on persons (as is claimed here for the accused,) without first obtaining the verdict of juries and the judgment of civil courts, then is this legislation a mockery, and the Constitution, which not only authorized but enjoined its enactment, but a glittering generality and a splendid bauble. Happily the Supreme Court has settled all controversy on this question. In speaking of the Rhode Island insurrection, the court say:

"The Constitution of the United States, as far as it has provided for an emergency of this kind and authorized the general government to interfere in the domestic concerns of a State, has treated the subject as political in its nature and placed the power in the hands of that department." * * *
"By the act of 1795 the power of deciding whether the exigency has arisen upon which the government of the United States is bound to interfere is given to the President."

The court add :

"When the President has acted and called out the militia, is a circuit court of the United States authorized to inquire whether his decision was right? If it could, then it would become the duty of the court, provided it came to the conclusion that the President had decided incorrectly, to discharge those who were arrested or detained by the troops in the service of the United States." * * * "If the judicial power extends so far, the guarantee contained in the Constitution of the United States is a guarantee of anarchy and not of order." * * * "Yet if this right does not reside in the courts when the conflict is raging, if the judicial power is at that time bound to follow the decision of the political, it must be equally bound when the contest is over. It cannot, when peace is restored, punish as offences and crimes the acts which it before recognized and was bound to recognize as lawful."— *Luther vs. Borden,* 7 Howard, 42, 43.

If this be law, what becomes of the volunteer advice of the volunteer counsel, by him given without money and without price, to this court, of their responsibility—their *personal* responsibility, for obeying the orders of the President of the United States in trying persons accused of the murder of the Chief Magistrate and commander-in-chief of the army and navy of the United States in time of rebellion, and in pursuance of a conspiracy entered into with the public enemy? I may be pardoned for asking the attention of the court to a further citation from this important decision, in which the court say, the employment of military power to put down an armed insurrection "is essential to the existence of every government, and is as necessary to the States of this Union as to any other government; and if the government of the State deem the armed opposition so formidable as to require the use of military force and the declaration of MARTIAL LAW, we see no ground upon which this court can question its authority." (*Ibid.*) This decision in terms declared that under the act of 1795 the President had power to decide and did decide the question so as to exclude further inquiry whether the State government which thus employed force and proclaimed martial law was the government of the State, and therefore was permitted to act. If a State may do this, to put down armed insurrection, may not the federal government as well? The reason of the man who doubts it may justly be questioned. I but quote the language of that tribunal, in another case before cited, when I say the Constitution confers upon the President the whole executive power.

We have seen that the proclamation of blockade made by the President was affirmed by the Supreme Court as a lawful and valid act, although its direct effect was to dispose of the property of whoever violated it, whether citizen or stranger. It is difficult to perceive what course of reasoning can be adopted, in the light of that decision, which will justify any man in saying that the President had not the like power to proclaim martial law in time of insurrection against the United States, and to establish, according to the customs of war among civilized nations, military tribunals of justice for its enforcement, and for the punishment of all crimes committed in the interests of the public enemy.

These acts of the President have, however, all been legalized by the subsequent legislation of Congress, although the Supreme Court decided, in relation to the proclamation of blockade, that no such legislation was necessary. By the act of August 6, 1861, ch. 63, sec. 3, it is enacted that—

"All the acts, proclamations, and orders of the President of the United States, after the 4th of March, 1861, respecting the army and navy of the United States, and calling out, or relating to, the militia or volunteers from the States, are hereby approved in all respects, legalized, and made valid to the same extent and with the same effect as if they had been issued and done under the previous express authority and direction of the Congress of the United States."—(12 Stat. at Large, 326.)

This act legalized, if any such legalization was necessary, all that the President had done from the day of his inauguration to that hour, in the prosecution of the war for the Union. He had suspended the privilege of the writ of habeas corpus, and resisted its execution when issued by the Chief Justice of the United States; he had called out and accepted the services of a large body of volunteers for a period not previously authorized by law; he had declared a blockade of the southern ports; he had declared the southern States in insurrection; he had ordered the armies to invade them and suppress it; thus exercising, in accordance with the laws of war, power over the life, the liberty, and the property of the citizens. Congress ratified it and affirmed it.

In like manner and by subsequent legislation did the Congress ratify and affirm the proclamation of martial law of September 25, 1862. That proclamation, as the court will have observed, declares that during the existing insurrection all rebels and insurgents, their aiders and abettors within the United States, and all persons guilty of any disloyal practice affording aid and comfort to the rebels against the authority of the United States, shall be subject to martial law and liable to trial and punishment by courts-martial or *military commission;* and second, that the writ of habeas corpus is suspended in respect to all persons arrested, or who are now, or hereafter during the rebellion shall be, imprisoned in any fort, &c., by any military authority, or by the sentence of any court-martial or *military commission.*

One would suppose that it needed no argument to satisfy an intelligent and patriotic citizen of the United States that, by the ruling of the Supreme Court cited, so much of this proclamation as declares that all rebels and insurgents, their aiders and abettors, shall be subject to martial law and be liable to trial and punishment by court-martial or military commission, needed no ratification by Congress. Every step that the President took against rebels and insurgents was taken in pursuance of the rules of war and was an exercise of martial law. Who says that he should not deprive them, by the authority of this law, of life and liberty? Are the aiders and abettors of these insurgents entitled to any higher consideration than the armed insurgents themselves? It is against these that the President proclaimed martial law, and against all others who were guilty of any disloyal practice affording aid and comfort to rebels against the authority of the United States. Against these he suspended the privilege of the writ of habeas corpus; and these, and only such as these, were by that proclamation subjected to trial and punishment by court-martial or military commission.

That the Proclamation covers the offence charged here, no man will, or dare, for a moment deny. Was it not a disloyal practice? Was it not aiding and abetting the insurgents and rebels to enter into a conspiracy with them to kill and murder, within your capital and your intrenched camp, the Commander-in-Chief of our army, your Lieutenant General, and the Vice-President, and the Secretary of State, with intent thereby to aid the rebellion, and subvert the Constitution and laws of the United States? But it is said that the President could not establish a court for their trial, and therefore Congress must ratify and affirm this Proclamation. I have said before that such an argument comes with ill grace from the lips of him who declared as solemnly that neither by the Congress nor by the President could either the rebel himself or his aider or abettor be lawfully and constitutionally subjected to trial by any military tribunal, whether court-martial or military commission. But the Congress did ratify, in the exercise of the power vested in them, every part of this Proclamation. I have said, upon the authority of the fathers of the Constitution, and of its judicial interpreters, that Congress has power by legislation to aid the Executive in the suppression of rebellion, in executing the laws of the Union when resisted by armed insurrection, and in repelling invasion.

By the act of March 3, 1863, the Congress of the United States, by the first section thereof, declared that during the present rebellion the President of the United States, whenever in his judgment the public safety may require it, is authorized to suspend the writ of habeas corpus in any case throughout the United States or any part thereof. By the fourth section of the same act it is declared that any order of the President, or under his authority, made at any time during the existence of the present rebellion, shall be a defence in all courts to any action or prosecution, civil or criminal, pending or to be commenced, for any search, seizure, arrest, or imprisonment, made, done, or committed, or acts omitted to be done, under and by virtue of such order. By the fifth section it is provided, that, if any suit or prosecution, civil or criminal, has been or shall be commenced in any State court against any officer, civil or military, or against any other person, for any arrest or imprisonment made, or other trespasses or wrongs done or committed, or any act omitted to be done at any time during the present rebellion, by virtue of or under color of any authority derived from or exercised by or under the President of the United States, if the defendant shall, upon appearance in such court, file a petition stating the facts upon affidavit, &c., as aforesaid, for the removal of the cause for trial to the circuit court of the United States, it shall be the duty of the State court, upon his giving security, to proceed no further in the cause or prosecution. Thus declaring that all orders of the President, made at any time during the existence of the present rebellion, and all acts done in pursuance thereof, shall be held valid in the courts of justice. Without further inquiry, these provisions of this statute embrace Order 141, which is the proclamation of martial law, and necessarily legalize every act done under it, either before the passage of the act of 1863 or since. Inasmuch as that Proclamation ordered that all rebels, insurgents, their aiders and abettors, and persons guilty of any disloyal practice affording aid and comfort to rebels against the authority of the United States, at any time during the existing insurrection, should be subject to martial law, and liable to trial and punishment by a *military commission*, the sections of the law just cited declaring lawful all acts done in pursuance of such order, including, of course, the trial and punishment by military commission of all such offenders, as directly legalized this order of the President as it is possible for Congress to legalize or authorize any executive act whatever. (12 Stat. at Large, 755–'6.)

But after assuming and declaring with great earnestness in his argument that no person could be tried and convicted for such crimes by any military tribunal, whether a court-martial or a military commission, save those in the land or naval service in time of war, the gentleman makes the extraordinary statement that the creation of a military commission must be authorized by the legislative department, and demands, if there be any such legislation, "let the statute be produced." The statute has been produced. The power so to try, says the gentleman, must be authorized by Congress, when the demand is made for such authority. Does not the gentleman thereby give up his argument, and admit, that if the Congress has so authorized the trial of all aiders and abettors of rebels or insurgents for whatever they do in aid of such rebels and insurgents during the insurrection, the statute and proceedings under it are lawful and valid? I have already shown that the Congress have so legislated by expressly legalizing Order No. 141, which directed the trial of all rebels, their aiders and abettors, by military commission. Did not Congress expressly legalize this order by declaring that the order shall be a defence in all courts to any action or prosecution, civil or criminal, for acts done in pursuance of it? No amount of argument could make this point clearer than the language of the statute itself. But, says the gentleman, if there be a statute authorizing trials by military commission, "Let it be produced."

By the act of March 3, 1863, it is provided in section thirty that in time of war, insurrection, or rebellion, murder and assault with intent to kill, &c., when committed by persons in the military service, shall be punishable by the sentence of a court-martial or *military commission*, and the punishment of such offences shall never be less than those inflicted by the laws of the State or District in which they may have been committed. By the 38th section of the same act, it is provided that all persons who, in time of war or rebellion against the United States, shall be found lurking or. acting as spies in or about the camps, &c., of the United States, or elsewhere, shall be triable by a *military commission*, and shall, upon conviction, suffer death. Here is a statute which expressly declares that all persons, whether citizens or strangers, who in time of rebellion shall be found acting as spies, shall suffer death upon conviction by a military commission. Why did not the gentleman give us some argument upon this law ? We have seen that it was the existing law of the United States under the Confederation. Then, and since, men not in the land or naval forces of the United States have suffered death for this offence upon conviction by courts-martial. If it was competent for Congress to authorize their trial by courts-martial, it was equally competent for Congress to authorize their trial by military commission, and accordingly they have done so. By the same authority the Congress may extend the jurisdiction of military commissions over all military offences or crimes committed in time of rebellion or war in aid of the public enemy ; and it certainly stands with right reason, that if it were just to subject to death, by the sentence of a military commission, all persons who should be guilty merely of lurking as spies in the interests of the public enemy in time of rebellion, though they obtained no information, though they inflicted no personal injury, but were simply overtaken and detected in the endeavor to obtain intelligence for the enemy, those who enter into conspiracy with the enemy, not only to lurk as spies in your camp, but to lurk there as murderers and assassins, and who, in pursuance of that conspiracy, commit assassination and murder upon the Commander-in-Chief of your army within your camp and in aid of rebellion, should be subject in like manner to trial by military commission. (Stat. at Large 12, 736-'7, ch. 8.)

Accordingly, the President having so declared, the Congress, as we have stated, have affirmed that his order was valid, and that all persons acting by authority, and consequently as a court pronouncing such sentence upon the offender as the usage of war requires, are justified by the law of the land. With all respect, permit me to say that the learned gentleman has manifested more acumen and ability in his elaborate argument by what he has omitted to say than by anything which he has said. By the act of July 2, 1864, cap. 215, it is provided that the commanding general in the field, or the commander of the department, as the case may be, shall have power to carry into execution all sentences against guerilla marauders for robbery, arson, burglary, &c., and for violation of the laws and customs of war, as well as sentences against spies, mutineers, deserters, and murderers.

From the legislation I have cited, it is apparent that military commissions are expressly recognized by the law-making power; that they are authorized to try capital offences against citizens not in the service of the United States, and to pronounce the sentence of death upon them; and that the commander of a department, or the commanding general in the field, may carry such sentence into execution. But, says the gentleman, grant all this to be so; Congress has not declared in what manner the court shall be constituted. The answer to that objection has already been anticipated in the citation from Benêt, wherein it appeared to be the rule of the law martial that in the punishment of all military offences not provided for by the written law of the land, military commissions are constituted for that purpose by the authority of the commanding officer or the Commander-in-Chief, as the case may be, who selects the officers of a court-martial; that they are similarly constituted, and their proceedings conducted according to the same general rules. That is a part of the very law martial which the President proclaimed, and which the Congress has legalized. The Proclamation has declared that all such offenders shall be tried by military commissions. The Congress has legalized the same by the act which I have cited; and by every intendment it must be taken that, as martial law is by the Proclamation declared to be the rule by which they shall be tried, the Congress, in affirming the act of the President, simply declared that they should be tried according to the customs of martial law; that the commission should be constituted by the Commander-in-Chief according to the rule of procedure known as martial law; and that the penalties inflicted should be in accordance with the laws of war and the usages of nations. Legislation no more definite than this has been upon your statute-book since the beginning of the century, and has been held by the Supreme Court of the United States valid for the punishment of offenders.

By the 32d article of the act of 23d April, 1800, it is provided that "all crimes committed by persons belonging to the navy which are not specified in the foregoing articles shall be punished according to the laws and customs in such cases at sea." Of this article the Supreme Court of the United States say, that when offences and crimes are not given in terms or by definition, the want of it may be supplied by a comprehensive enactment such as the 32d article of the rules for the government of the navy; which means that courts-martial have jurisdiction of such crimes as are not specified, but which have been recognized to be crimes and offences by the usages in the navies of all nations, and that they shall be punished according to the laws and customs of the sea. (Dynes vs. Hoover, 20 Howard, 82.)

But it is a fact that must not be omitted in the reply which I make to the gentleman's argument, that an effort was made by himself and others in the Senate of the United States, on the 3d of March last, to condemn the arrests, imprisonments, &c., made by order of the President of the United States in pursuance of his proclamation, and to reverse, by the judgment of that body, the law which had been before passed affirming his action, which effort most signally failed.

Thus we see that the body which by the Constitution, if the President had been guilty of the misdemeanors alleged against him in this argument of the gentleman, would, upon presentation of such charge in legal form against the President, constitute the high court of impeachment for his trial and condemnation, has decided the question in advance, and declared upon the occasion referred to, as they had before declared by solemn enactment, that this order of the President declaring martial law and the punishment of all rebels and insurgents, their aiders and abettors, by military commission, should be enforced during the insurrection, as the law of the land, and that the offenders should be tried, as directed, by military commission. It may be said that this subsequent legislation of Congress, ratifying and affirming what had been done by the President, can have no validity. Of course it cannot if neither the Congress nor the Executive can authorize the proclamation and enforcement of martial law in the suppression of rebellion for the punishment of all persons committing military offences in aid of that rebellion. Assuming, however, as the gentleman seemed to assume, by asking for the legislation of Congress, that there is such power in Congress, the Supreme Court of the United States has solemnly affirmed that such ratification is valid. (2 Black, 671.)

The gentleman's argument is full of citations of English precedent. There is a late English precedent bearing upon this point—the power of the legislature, by subsequent enactment, to legalize executive orders, arrests, and imprisonment of citizens—that I beg leave to commend to his consideration. I refer to the statute of 11 and 12

Victoria, ch. 35, entitled "An act to empower the lord lieutenant, or other chief governor or governors of Ireland, to apprehend and detain until the first day of March, 1849, such persons as he or they shall *suspect* of conspiring against her Majesty's person and government," passed July 25, 1848, which statute in terms declares that all and every person and persons who is, are, or shall be, within that period, within that part of the United Kingdom of England and Ireland called Ireland at or on the day the act shall receive her Majesty's royal assent, or after, by warrant for high treason or treasonable practices, or *suspicion* of high treason or treasonable practices, signed by the lord lieutenant, or other chief governor or governors of Ireland for the time being, or his or their chief secretary, for such causes as aforesaid, may be detained in safe custody without bail or main prize, until the first day of March, 1849; and that no judge or justice shall bail or try any such person or persons so committed, without order from her Majesty's privy council, until the said first day of March, 1849, any law or statute to the contrary notwithstanding. The 2d section of this act provides that, in cases where any persons have been, *before* the passing of the act, arrested, committed, or detained for such cause by warrant or warrants signed by the officers aforesaid, or either of them, it may be lawful for the person or persons to whom such warrants have been or shall be directed, to detain such person or persons in his or their custody in any place whatever in Ireland; and that such person or persons to whom such warrants have been or shall be directed shall be deemed and taken, to all intents and purposes, lawfully authorized to take into safe custody and be the lawful jailers and keepers of such persons so arrested, committed, or detained.

Here the power of arrest is given by the act of Parliament to the governor or his secretary; the process of the civil courts was wholly suspended; bail was denied and the parties imprisoned, and this not by process of the courts, but by warrant of a chief governor or his secretary; not for crimes charged to have been committed, but for being *suspected* of treasonable practices. Magna charta it seems opposes no restraint, notwithstanding the parade that is made about it in this argument, upon the power of the Parliament of England to legalize arrests and imprisonments made before the passage of the act upon an executive order, and without colorable authority of statute law, and to authorize like arrests and imprisonments of so many of six million of people as such executive officers might *suspect* of treasonable practices.

But, says the gentleman, whatever may be the precedents, English or American, whatever may be the provisions of the Constitution, whatever may be the legislation of Congress, whatever may be the proclamations and orders of the President as commander-in-chief, it is a usurpation and a tyranny in time of rebellion and civil war to subject any citizen to trial for any crime before military tribunals, save such citizens as are in the land or naval forces, and against this usurpation, which he asks this court to rebuke by solemn decision, he appeals to public opinion. I trust that I set as high value upon enlightened public opinion as any man. I recognize it as the reserved power of the people which creates and dissolves armies, which creates and dissolves legislative assemblies, which enacts and repeals fundamental laws, the better to provide for personal security by the due administration of justice. To that public opinion upon this very question of the usurpation of authority, of unlawful arrests, and unlawful imprisonments, and unlawful trials, condemnations, and executions by the late President of the United States, an appeal has already been taken. On this very issue the President was tried before the tribunal of the people, that great nation of freemen who cover this continent, looking out upon Europe from their eastern and upon Asia from their western homes. That people came to the consideration of this issue not unmindful of the fact that the first struggle for the establishment of our nationality could not have been, and was not, successfully prosecuted without the proclamation and enforcement of martial law, declaring, as we have seen, that any inhabitant who, during that war, should kill any loyal citizen, or enter into any combination for that purpose, should, upon trial and conviction before a military tribunal, be sentenced as an assassin, traitor, or spy, and should suffer death, and that in this last struggle for the maintenance of American nationality the President but followed the example of the illustrious Father of his Country. Upon that issue the people passed judgment on the 8th day of last November, and declared that the charge of usurpation was false.

From this decision of the people there lies no appeal on this earth. Who can rightfully challenge the authority of the American people to decide such questions for themselves? The voice of the people, thus solemnly proclaimed, by the omnipotence of the ballot, in favor of the righteous order of their murdered President, issued by him for the common defence, for the preservation of the Constitution, and for the enforcement of the laws of the Union, ought to be accepted, and will be accepted, I trust, by all just men, as the voice of God.

MAY IT PLEASE THE COURT: I have said thus much touching the right of the people, under their Constitution, in time of civil war and rebellion, to proclaim through their Executive, with the sanction and approval of their Congress, martial law, and enforce the same according to the usage of nations.

I submit that it has been shown that, by the letter and spirit of the Constitution, as well as by its contemporaneous construction, followed and approved by every department of the government, this right is in the people; that it is inseparable from the condition of war, whether civil or foreign, and absolutely essential to its vigorous and successful prosecution ; that according to the highest authority upon constitutional law, the proclamation and enforcement of martial law are "usual under all governments in time of rebellion;" that our own highest judicial tribunal has declared this, and solemnly ruled that the question of the necessity for its exercise rests exclusively with Congress and the President ; and that the decision of the political departments of the government, that there is an armed rebellion and a necessity for the employment of military force and martial law in its suppression, concludes the judiciary.

In submitting what I have said in support of the jurisdiction of this honorable court, and of its constitutional power to hear and determine this issue, I have uttered my own convictions; and for their utterance in defence of my country, and its right to employ all the means necessary for the common defence against armed rebellion and secret treasonable conspiracy in aid of such rebellion, I shall neither ask pardon nor offer apology. I find no words with which more fitly to conclude all I have to say upon the question of the jurisdiction and constitutional authority of this court than those employed by the illustrious Lord Brougham to the House of Peers in support of the bill before referred to, which empowered the lord lieutenant of Ireland, and his deputies, to apprehend and detain, for the period of seven months or more, all such persons within that island as they should *suspect* of conspiracy against her Majesty's person and government. Said that illustrious man : "A friend of liberty I have lived, and such will I die ; nor care I how soon the latter event may happen, if I cannot be a friend of liberty without being a friend of traitors at the same time—a protector of criminals of the deepest dye—an accomplice of foul rebellion and of its concomitant, civil war, with all its atrocities and all its fearful consequences." (Hansard's Debates, 3d series, vol. 100, p. 635.)

MAY IT PLEASE THE COURT: It only remains for me to sum up the evidence, and present my views of the law arising upon the facts in the case on trial. The questions of fact involved in the issue are:

First, did the accused, or any two of them, confederate and conspire together as charged? and—

Second, did the accused, or any of them, in pursuance of such conspiracy, and with the intent alleged, commit either or all of the several acts specified?

If the conspiracy be established, as laid, it results that whatever was said or done by either of the parties thereto, in the furtherance or execution of the common design, is the declaration or act of all the other parties to the conspiracy; and this, whether the other parties, at the time such words were uttered or such acts done by their confederates, were present or absent—here, within the intrenched lines of your capital, or crouching behind the intrenched lines of Richmond, or awaiting the results of their murderous plot against their country, its Constitution and laws, across the border, under the shelter of the British flag.

The declared and accepted rule of law in cases of conspiracy is that—

"In prosecutions for conspiracy it is an established rule that where several persons are proved to have combined together for the same illegal purpose, any act done by one of the party, in pursuance of the original concerted plan, and in reference to the common object, is, in the contemplation of law as well as in sound reason, the act of the whole party; and, therefore, the proof of the act will be evidence against any of the others, who were engaged in the same general conspiracy, without regard to the question whether the prisoner is proved to have been concerned in the particular transaction." (Phillips on Evidence, p. 210.)

The same rule obtains in cases of treason: "If several persons agree to levy war, some in one place and some in another, and one party do actually appear in arms, this is a levying of war by all, as well those who were not in arms as those who were, if it were done in pursuance of the original concert, for those who made the attempt were emboldened by the confidence inspired by the general concert, and therefore these particular acts are in justice imputable to all the rest." (1 East., Pleas of the Crown, p. 97; Roscoe, 84.)

In *Ex parte Bollman and Swartwout*, 4 Cranch, 126, Marshall, Chief Justice, rules: "If war be actually levied—that is, if a body of men be actually assembled, for the purpose of effecting, by force, a treasonable purpose, all those who perform any part, *however minute, or however remote from the scene of action*, and who are actually leagued in the general conspiracy, are to be considered as traitors."

In *United States* vs. *Cole et al.*, 5 McLean, 601, Mr. Justice McLean says: "A conspiracy is rarely, if ever, proved by positive testimony. When a crime of high magnitude is about to be perpetrated by a combination of individuals, they do not act openly but covertly and secretly. The purpose formed is known only to those who enter into it. Unless one of the original conspirators betray his companions and give evidence against them, their guilt can be proved only by circumstantial evidence. * * It is said by some writers on evidence that such circumstances are stronger than positive proof. A witness swearing positively, it is said, may misapprehend the facts or swear falsely, but that circumstances cannot lie.

"The common design is the essence of the charge ; and this may be made to appear when the defendants steadily pursue the same object, whether acting separately or together, by common or different means, all leading to the same unlawful result. And where *prima facie* evidence has been given of a combination, the acts or confessions of one are evidence against all. * * It is reasonable that where a body of men assume the attribute of individuality, whether for commercial business or for the commission of a crime, that the association should be bound by the acts of one of its members, in carrying out the design."

It is a rule of the law, not to be overlooked in this connexion, that the conspiracy or agreement of the parties, or some of them, to act in concert to accomplish the unlawful act charged, may be established either by direct evidence of a meeting or consultation for the illegal purpose charged, or more usually, from the very nature of the case, by circumstantial evidence. (2 Starkie, 232.)

Lord Mansfield ruled that it was not necessary to prove the actual fact of a conspiracy, but that it might be collected from collateral circumstances. (Parson's Case, 1 W. Blackstone, 392.)

"If," says a great authority on the law of evidence, "on a charge of conspiracy, it appear that two persons by their acts are pursuing the same object, and often by the same means, or one performing part of the act, and the other completing it, for the attainment of the same object, the jury may draw the conclusion there is a conspiracy. If a conspiracy be formed, and a person join in it afterwards, he is equally guilty with the original conspirators." (Roscoe, 415.)

"The rule of the admissibility of the acts and declarations of any one of the conspirators, said or done in furtherance of the common design, applies in cases as well where only part of the conspirators are indicted, or upon trial, as where all are indicted and upon trial. Thus, upon an indictment for murder, if it appear that others, together with the prisoner, conspired to commit the crime, the act of one, done in pursuance of that intention, will be evidence against the rest." (2d Starkie, 237.)

They are all alike guilty as principals. (Commonwealth vs. Knapp, 9 Pickering, 496; 10 Pickering, 477; 6 Term Reports, 528; 11 East., 584.)

What is the evidence, direct and circumstantial, that the accused, or either of them, together with John H. Surratt, John Wilkes Booth, Jefferson Davis, George N. Sanders, Beverley Tucker, Jacob Thompson, William C. Cleary, Clement C. Clay, George Harper, and George Young, did combine, confederate, and conspire, in aid of the existing rebellion, as charged, to kill and murder, within the military department of Washington, and within the fortified and intrenched lines thereof, Abraham Lincoln, late, and, at the time of the said combining, confederating, and conspiring, President of the United States of America and commander-in-chief of the army and navy thereof; Andrew Johnson, Vice President of the United States; William H. Seward, Secretary of State of the United States; and Ulysses S. Grant, lieutenant general of the armies thereof, and then in command, under the direction of the President?

The time, as laid in the charge and specification, when this conspiracy was entered into, is immaterial, so that it appear by the evidence that the criminal combination and agreement were formed before the commission of the acts alleged. That Jefferson Davis, one of the conspirators named, was the acknowledged chief and leader of the existing rebellion against the government of the United States. and that Jacob Thompson, George N. Sanders, Clement C. Clay, Beverley Tucker, and others named in the specification, were his duly accredited and authorized agents to act in the interests of said rebellion, are facts established by the testimony in this case beyond all question. That Davis, as the leader of said rebellion, gave to those agents, then in Canada, commissions in blank, bearing the official signature of his war minister, James A. Seddon, to be by them filled up and delivered to such agents as they might employ to act in the interests of the rebellion within the United States, and intended to be a cover and protection for any crimes they might therein commit in the service of the rebellion, is also a fact established here, and which no man can gainsay. Who doubts that Kennedy, whose confession, made in view of immediate death, as proved here, was commissioned by those accredited agents of Davis to burn the city of New York?—that he was to have attempted it on the night of the presidential election, and that he did, in combination with his confederates, set fire to four hotels in the city of New York on the night of the 25th of November last? Who doubts that, in like manner, in the interests of the rebellion and by the authority of Davis, these his agents also commissioned Bennett H. Young to commit arson, robbery, and the murder of unarmed citizens, in St. Albans, Vermont? Who doubts, upon the testimony shown, that Davis, by his agents, deliberately adopted the system of starvation for the murder of our captive soldiers in his hands; or that, as shown by the testimony, he sanctioned the burning of hospitals and steamboats, the property of private persons, and paid therefor from his stolen treasure the sum of thirty-five thousand dollars in gold? By the evidence of Joseph Godfrey Hyams it is proved that Thompson—the agent of Jefferson Davis—paid him money for the service he rendered in the infamous and fiendish project of importing pestilence into our camps and cities to destroy the lives of citizens and soldiers alike, and into the house of the President for the purpose of destroying his life. It may be said, and doubtless will be said, by the pensioned advocates of this rebellion, that Hyams, being infamous, is not to be believed. It is admitted that he is infamous, as it must be conceded that any man is infamous who either participates in such a crime or attempts in anywise to extenuate it. But it will be observed that Hyams is supported by the testimony of Mr. Sanford Conover, who heard Blackburn and the other rebel agents in Canada speak of this infernal project, and by the testimony of Mr. Wall, the well-known auctioneer of this city, whose character is unquestioned, that he received this importation of pestilence, (of course without any knowledge of the purpose,) and that Hyams consigned the goods to him in the name of J. W. Harris— a fact in itself an acknowledgment of guilt; and that he received afterwards a letter from Harris, dated Toronto, Canada West, December 1, 1864, wherein Harris stated that he had not been able to come to the States since his return to Canada, and asked for an account of the sale. He identifies the Godfrey Joseph Hyams who testified in court as the J. W. Harris who imported the pestilence. The very transaction shows that Hyams's statement is truthful. He gives the names of the parties connected with this infamy, (Clement C. Clay, Dr. Blackburn, Rev. Dr. Stuart Robinson, J. C. Holcombe—all refugees from the confederacy in Canada,) and states that he gave Thompson a receipt for the fifty dollars paid to him, and that he was by occupation a shoemaker; in none of which facts is there an attempt to discredit him. It is not probable that a man in his position in life would be able to buy five trunks of clothing, ship them all the way from Halifax to Washington, and then order them to be sold at auction, without regard to price, solely upon his own account. It is a matter of notoriety that a part of his statement is verified by the results at Newbern, North Carolina, to which point, he says, a portion of the infected goods were shipped, through a sutler; the result of which was, that nearly two thousand citizens and soldiers died there about that time with the yellow fever.

That the rebel chief, Jefferson Davis, sanctioned these crimes, committed and attempted through the instrumentality of his accredited agents in Canada—Thompson, Clay, Tucker, Sanders, Cleary, &c.—upon the persons and property of the people of the north, there is positive proof on your record. The letter brought from Richmond; and taken from the archives of his late pretended government there; dated February 11, 1865, and addressed to him by a late rebel senator from Texas, W. S. Oldham, contains the following significant words: "When senator Johnson, of Missouri, and myself waited on you a few days since, in relation to the project of annoying and harassing the enemy by means of burning their shipping, towns, &c., &c., there were several remarks made by you upon the subject, which I was not fully prepared to answer, but which, upon subsequent conference with parties proposing the enterprise, I find cannot apply as objections to the scheme. First, the 'combustible materials' consist of several preparations, and not one alone, and can be used without exposing the party using them to the least danger of detection whatever. * * * Second, there is no necessity for sending persons in the military service into the enemy's country, but the work may be done by agents. * * * I have seen enough of the effects that can be produced to satisfy me that in most cases, without any danger to the parties engaged, and in others but very slight, we can, first, burn every vessel that leaves a foreign port for the United States; second, we can burn every transport that leaves the harbor of New York, or other northern port, with supplies for the armies of the enemy in the south; third, burn every transport and gunboat on the Mississippi river, as well as devastate the country of the enemy, and fill his people with terror and consternation. * * * For the purpose of satisfying your mind upon the subject, I respectfully, but earnestly, request that you will give an interview with General Harris, formerly a member of Congress from Missouri, who, I think, is able, from conclusive proofs, to convince you that what I have suggested is perfectly feasible and practicable."

No one can doubt, from the tenor of this letter, that the rebel Davis only wanted to be satisfied that this system of arson and murder could be carried on by his agents in the north successfully and without detection. With him it was not a crime to do these acts, but only a crime to be detected in them. But Davis, by his indorsement on this letter, dated the 20th of February, 1865, bears witness to his own complicity and his own infamy in this proposed work of destruction and crime for the future, as well as to his complicity in what had before been attempted without complete success. Kennedy, with his confederates, had failed to burn the city of New York. "The combustibles" which Kennedy had employed were, it seems, defective. This was "a difficulty to be overcome." Neither had he been able to consummate the dreadful work without subjecting himself *to detection.* This was another "*difficulty* to be overcome." Davis, on the 20th of February, 1865, indorsed upon this letter these words: "Secretary of State, at his convenience, see General Harris and learn what plan he has for *overcoming the difficulties heretofore experienced. J. D.*"

This indorsement is unquestionably proved to be the handwriting of Jefferson Davis, and it bears witness on its face that the monstrous proposition met his approval, and that he desired his rebel Secretary of State, Benjamin, to see General Harris and learn how to overcome *the difficulty heretofore experienced*, to wit: the inefficiency of "the combustible materials" that had been employed, and the liability of his agents to detection. After this, who will doubt that he had endeavored, by the hand of incendiaries, to destroy by fire the property and lives of the people of the north, and thereby "fill them with terror and consternation;" that he knew his agents had been unsuccessful; that he knew his agents had been detected in their villany and punished for their crime; that he desired through a more perfect "chemical preparation," by the science and skill of Professor McCulloch, to accomplish successfully what had before been unsuccessfully attempted?

The intercepted letter of his **agent**, Clement C. Clay, dated St.

Catherine's, Canada West, November 1, 1864, is an acknowledgment and confession of what they had attempted, and a suggestion made through J. P. Benjamin, rebel Secretary of State, of what remained to be done, in order to make the "chemical preparations" efficient. Speaking of this Bennett H. Young, he says: "You have doubtless learned through the press of the United States of the raid on St. Albans by about twenty-five confederate soldiers, led by Lieutenant Bennett H. Young; of their attempt and failure to burn the town; of their robbery of three banks there of the aggregate amount of about two hundred thousand dollars; of their arrest in Canada, by United States forces; of their commitment and the pending preliminary trial." He makes application, in aid of Young and his associates, for additional documents, showing that they acted upon the authority of the Confederate States government, taking care to say, however, that he held such authority at the time, but that it ought to be more explicit, so far as regards the particular acts complained of. He states that he met Young at Halifax in May, 1864, who developed his plans for retaliation on the enemy; that he, Clay, recommended him to the rebel Secretary of War; that after this "Young was sent back by the Secretary of War with a commission as second lieutenant to execute his plans and purposes, but to report to Hon. —— and myself." Young afterwards "proposed passing through New England, burning some towns and robbing them of whatever he could convert to the use of the confederate government. This I approved as justifiable retaliation. He attempted to burn the town of St. Albans, Vermont, and would have succeeded but for the failure of the *chemical preparation* with which he was armed. He then robbed the banks of funds amounting to over two hundred thousand dollars. That he was not prompted by selfish or mercenary motives I am as well satisfied as I am that he is an honest man. He assured me before going that his effort would be to destroy towns and farmhouses, but not to plunder or rob; but he said if, after firing a town, he saw he could take *funds* from a bank or any house, and thereby might inflict injury upon the enemy and benefit his own government, he would do so. He added most emphatically, that *whatever* he took should be turned over to the government or *its representatives in foreign lands*. My instructions to him were, to destroy whatever was valuable; not to stop to rob, but if, after firing a town, he could seize and carry off money or treasury or bank notes, he might do so upon condition that they were delivered to the proper authorities of the Confederate States"—that is, to Clay himself.

When he wrote this letter it seems that this accredited agent of

Jefferson Davis was as strongly impressed with the *usurpation and despotism* of Mr. Lincoln's administration as some of *the advocates* of his aiders and abettors seem to be at this day ; and he indulges in the following statement : "All that a large portion of the northern people, especially in the northwest, want to resist the *oppressions* of the *despotism* at Washington is a *leader*. They are ripe for resistance, *and it may come soon after the presidential election*. At all events, it must come, if our armies are not overcome, or destroyed, or dispersed. No people of the Anglo-Saxon blood can long endure *the usurpations and tyrannies of Lincoln.*" Clay does not sign the despatch, but indorses the bearer of it as a person who can identify him and give his name. The bearer of that letter was the witness Richard Montgomery, who saw Clay write a portion of the letter, and received it from his hands, and subsequently delivered it to the Assistant Secretary of War of the United States, Mr. Dana. That the letter is in Clay's handwriting is clearly proved by those familiar with it. Mr. Montgomery testifies that he was instructed by Clay to deliver this letter to Benjamin, the rebel Secretary of State, if he could get through to Richmond, and to tell him what names to put in the blanks.

This letter leaves no doubt, if any before existed in the mind of any one who had read the letter of Oldham and Davis's indorsement thereon, that "the chemical preparations" and "combustible materials" had been tried and had failed, and it had become a matter of great moment and concern that they should be so prepared as, in the words of Davis, "to overcome the difficulties heretofore experienced ;" that is to say, complete the work of destruction, and secure the perpetrators against personal injury or detection in the performance of it.

It only remains to be seen whether Davis, the procurer of arson and of the indiscriminate murder of the innocent and unoffending necessarily resultant therefrom, was capable also of endeavoring to procure, and in fact did procure, the murder, by direct assassination, of the President of the United States and others charged with the duty of maintaining the government of the United States, and of suppressing the rebellion in which this arch-traitor and conspirator was engaged.

The official papers of Davis, captured under the guns of our victorious army in his rebel capital, identified beyond question or shadow of doubt, and placed upon your record, together with the declarations and acts of his co-conspirators and agents, proclaim to all the world that he was capable of attempting to accomplish his treasonable procuration of the murder of the late President, and other chief officers of the United States, by the hands of hired assassins.

In the fall of 1864 Lieutenant W. Alston addresses to "his excellency" a letter now before the court, which contains the following words:

"I now offer you my services, and if you will favor *me in my designs*, I will proceed, as soon as my health will permit, to rid *my* country of some of her deadliest enemies, by striking at the very *hearts' blood* of those who seek to enchain her in slavery. I consider nothing *dishonorable* having such a tendency. All I ask of you is, to favor me by granting me the necessary papers, &c., to travel on. * * * *
I am perfectly familiar with the north, and feel confident that I can *execute* anything I undertake. I was in the raid last June in Kentucky, under General John H. Morgan; * * * was taken prisoner; * * * escaped from them by dressing myself in the garb of a citizen. * * * I went through to the Canadas, from whence, by the assistance of *Colonel J. P. Holcomb*, I succeeded in working my way around and through the blockade. * * * I should like to have a *personal* interview with you in order to perfect the arrangements before starting."

Is there any room to doubt that this was a proposition to *assassinate*, by the hand of this man and his associates, such persons in the north as he deemed the "deadliest enemies" of the rebellion? The weakness of the man who for a moment can doubt that such was the proposition of the writer of this letter is certainly an object of commiseration. What had Jefferson Davis to say to this proposed assassination of the "deadliest enemies" in the north of his great treason? Did the atrocious suggestion kindle in him indignation against the villain who offered, with his own hand, to strike the blow? Not at all. On the contrary, he ordered his private secretary, on the 29th of November, 1864, to indorse upon the letter these words: "Lieutenant W. Alston; accompanied raid into Kentucky, and was captured, but escaped into *Canada*, from whence he found his way back. Now offers his services to rid the country of some of its *deadliest enemies;* asks for papers, &c. Respectfully referred, by direction of the President, to the honorable Secretary of War." It is also indorsed, for attention, "By order. (Signed) J. A. Campbell, Assistant Secretary of War."

Note the fact in this connexion, that Jefferson Davis himself, as well as his subordinates, had, before the date of this indorsement, concluded that Abraham Lincoln was "the deadliest enemy" of the rebellion. You hear it in the rebel camp in Virginia in 1863, declared by Booth. then and there present, and assented to by rebel officers, that "Abraham Lincoln must be killed." You hear it in that slaughter-pen in Georgia, Andersonville, proclaimed among rebel officers, who, by the slow torture of starvation, inflicted cruel and untimely death on ten thousand of your defenders, captives in their hands—whispering, like demons, their horrid purpose, "Abraham Lincoln must be killed." And in Canada, the accredited agents of Jefferson Davis, as early as October, 1864, and afterwards, declared that "Abraham Lincoln must be killed" if his re-election could not be prevented. These agents in Canada, on the 13th of October, 1864, delivered, in cipher, to be transmitted to Richmond by Richard Montgomery, the witness, whose reputation is unchallenged, the following communication :

"OCTOBER 13, 1864.

"We again urge the immense necessity of our gaining immediate advantages. Strain every nerve for victory. We now look upon the re-election of *Lincoln* in November as almost certain, and we need to whip his hirelings to prevent it. Besides, with *Lincoln* re-elected, and his armies victorious, we need not hope even for recognition, much less the help mentioned in our last. Holcomb will explain this. Those figures of the Yankee armies are correct to a unit. *Our friends shall be immediately set to work as you direct.*"

To which an official reply, in cipher, was delivered to Montgomery by an agent of the state department in Richmond, dated October 19, 1864, as follows :

"Your letter of the 13th instant is at hand. There is yet time enough to colonize many *voters* before November. A blow will shortly be stricken here. It is not quite time. General Longstreet is to attack Sheridan without delay, and then move north as far as practicable toward unprotected points. This will be made instead of movement before mentioned. He will endeavor to assist the *republicans* in *collecting their ballots.* Be watchful and assist him."

On the very day of the date of this Richmond despatch Sheridan was attacked, with what success history will declare. The court will not fail to notice that the *re-election of Mr. Lincoln* is to be prevented if possible, by any and every means. Nor will they fail to notice that *Holcomb* is to "explain this"—the same person who, in Canada, was the friend and advisor of *Alston*, who proposed to Davis the assassination of the "deadliest enemies" of the rebellion.

In the despatch of the 13th of October, which was borne by Montgomery, and transmitted to Richmond in October last, you will find these words : "Our friends shall be immediately set to work as you direct." Mr. Lincoln is the subject of that despatch. Davis is therein notified that his agents in Canada look upon the re-election of Mr. Lincoln in November as almost certain. In this connexion he is assured by those agents, that the *friends* of their cause are to be set to work as Davis *had directed*. The conversations, which are proved by witnesses whose character stands unimpeached, disclose what "work" the "friends" were to do under *the direction* of Davis himself. Who were these "friends," and what was "the work" which his agents, Thompson, Clay, Tucker and Sanders had been directed to set them at ? Let Thompson answer for himself. In a conversation with Richard Montgomery in the summer of 1864, Thompson said that "he *had his friends,* confederates, all over the northern States, who were ready and willing to go any lengths for the good of the cause of the south, and he could at any time have the *tyrant Lincoln,* or *any other of his advisers* that he chose, *put out of his way;* that they would not consider it *a crime* when done for the cause of the confederacy." This conversation was repeated by the witness in the summer of 1864 to Clement C. Clay, who immediately stated : "That is so ; we are all devoted to our cause and ready to go any length—to do anything under the sun."

At and about the time that these declarations of Clay and Thompson were made, *Alston,* who made the proposition, as we have seen, to Davis, to be furnished with papers *to go north* and rid the confederacy of some of its "deadliest enemies," was in Canada. He was doubtless one of the "friends" referred to. As appears by the testimony of Montgomery, Payne, the prisoner at your bar, was about that time in Canada, and was seen standing by Thompson's door, engaged in a conversation with Clay, between whom and the witness some words were interchanged, when Clay stated he (Payne) was one of *their friends*—"we trust him." It is proved beyond a shadow of doubt that in October last John Wilkes Booth, the assassin of the President, was also in Canada and upon intimate terms with Thompson, Clay, Sanders, and other rebel agents. Who can doubt, in the light of the events which have since transpired, that he was one of the "friends" to be "set to work," as Davis had already directed--not, perhaps, as yet to assassinate the President, but to do that other work which is suggested in the letter of Oldham, indorsed by Davis in his own hand, and spread upon your record—the work of the secret incendiary, which was to "fill the people of the north with terror and consternation." The other "work" spoken of by Thompson—putting the *tyrant Lincoln* and *any of his advisers out of the way*, was work doubtless to be commenced only after the re-election of Mr. Lincoln, which they had already declared in their despatch to their employer, Davis, was with them a foregone conclusion. At all events, it was not until after the presidential election in November that Alston proposed to Davis to go north on the work of assassination; nor was it until after that election that Booth was found in possession of the letter which is in evidence, and which discloses the purpose to assassinate the President. Being assured, however, when Booth was with them in Canada, as they had already declared in their despatch, that the re-election of Mr. Lincoln was certain, in which event there would be no hope for the confederacy, they doubtless entered into the arrangement with Booth as one of their "friends," that as soon as that fact was determined he should go "to work," and as soon as might be "rid the confederacy of the tyrant Lincoln and of his advisers."

That these persons named upon your record, Thompson, Sanders, Clay, Cleary, and Tucker, were the agents of Jefferson Davis, is another fact established in this case beyond a doubt. They made affidavit of it themselves, of record here, upon the examination of their "friends," charged with the raid upon St. Albans, before Judge Smith, in Canada. It is in evidence also by the letter of Clay, before referred to.

The testimony, to which I have thus briefly referred, shows, by the letter of his agents, of the 13th of October, that Davis had before directed those agents to set his *friends to work*. By the letter of Clay it seems that his direction had been obeyed, and his friends had been set to work, in the burning and robbery and murder at St. Albans, in the attempt to burn the city of New York, and in the attempt to introduce pestilence into this capital and into the house of the President. It having appeared, by the letter of Alston, and the indorsement thereon, that Davis had in November entertained the proposition of sending agents, that is to say, "friends," to the north to not only "spread terror and consternation among the people" by means of his "chemical preparations," but also, in the words of that letter, "to strike," by the hands of assassins, "at the heart's blood" of the deadliest enemies in the north to the confederacy of traitors ;

it has also appeared by the testimony of many respectable witnesses, among others the attorneys who represented the people of the United States and the State of Vermont, in the preliminary trial of the raiders in Canada, that Clay, Thompson, Tucker, Sanders and Cleary declared themselves the agents of the confederacy. It also clearly appears by the correspondence referred to, and the letter of Clay, that they were holding, and at any time able to command, blank commissions from Jefferson Davis to authorize *their friends* to do whatever work they appointed them to do, in the interests of the rebellion, by the destruction of life and property in the north.

If a *prima facie* case justifies, as we have seen by the law of evidence it does, the introduction of all declarations and acts of any of the parties to a conspiracy, uttered or done in the prosecution of the common design, as evidence against all the rest, it results, that whatever was said or done in furtherance of the common design, after this month of October, 1864, by either of these agents in Canada, is evidence not only against themselves, but against Davis as well, of his complicity with them in the conspiracy.

Mr. Montgomery testifies that he met Jacob Thompson in January, at Montreal, when he said that "a proposition had been made to him to rid the world of the tyrant Lincoln, Stanton, Grant, and some others ; that he knew the men who had made the proposition were bold, daring men, able to execute what they undertook; that he himself was in favor of the proposition, but had determined to defer his answer until he had consulted his government at Richmond ; that he was then only awaiting their approval." This was about the middle of January, and consequently more than a month after Alston had made his proposition direct to Davis, in writing, to go north and rid their confederacy of some of its "deadliest enemies." It was at the time of this conversation that Payne, the prisoner, was seen by the witness standing at Thompson's door in conversation with Clay. This witness also shows the intimacy between Thompson, Clay, Cleary, Tucker, and Sanders.

A few days after the assassination of the President, Beverley Tucker said to this witness "that President Lincoln deserved his death long ago ; that it was a pity he didn't have it long ago, and it was too bad that the boys had not been allowed to act when they wanted to."

This remark undoubtedly had reference to the propositions made in the fall to Thompson, and also to Davis, to rid the south of its deadliest enemies by their assassination. Cleary, who was accredited by Thompson as his confidential agent, also stated to this witness that Booth was one of the party to whom Thompson had referred in the conversation in January, in which he said he knew the men who were ready to rid the world of the tyrant Lincoln, and of Stanton and Grant. Cleary also said, speaking of the assassination, "that it was a pity that the whole work had not been done," and added, "they had better look out—we are not done yet;" manifestly referring to the statement made by his employer, Thompson, before in the summer, that not only the tyrant Lincoln, but Stanton and Grant, and others of his advisers, should be put out of the way. Cleary also stated to this witness that Booth had visited Thompson twice in the winter, the last time in December, and had also been there in the summer.

Sanford Conover testified that he had been for some time a clerk in the war department at Richmond; that in Canada he knew Thompson, Sanders, Cleary, Tucker, Clay, and other rebel agents; that he knew John H. Surratt and John Wilkes Booth; that he saw Booth there upon one occasion, and Surratt upon several successive days; that he saw Surratt (whom he describes) in April last, in Thompson's room, and also in company with Sanders; that about the 6th or 7th of April Surratt delivered to Jacob Thompson a despatch brought by him from Benjamin at Richmond, enclosing one in cipher from Davis. Thompson had before this proposed to Conover to engage in a plot to assassinate President Lincoln and his cabinet, and on this occasion he laid his hand upon these despatches and said, "This makes the thing all right," referring to the assent of the rebel authorities, and stated that the rebel authorities had consented to the plot to assassinate Lincoln, Johnson, the Secretary of War, Secretary of State, Judge Chase, and General Grant. Thompson remarked further that the assassination of these parties would leave the government of the United States entirely without a head; that there was no provision in the Constitution of the United States by which they could elect another President, if these men were put out of the way.

In speaking of this assassination of the President and others, Thompson said that it was only removing them from office, that the killing of a tyrant was no murder. It seems that he had learned precisely the same lesson that Alston had learned in November, when he communicated with Davis, and said, speaking of the President's assassination, "he did not think anything dishonorable that would serve their cause." Thompson stated at the same time that he had conferred a commission on Booth, and that everybody engaged in the enterprise would be commissioned, and if it succeeded, or failed, and they escaped into Canada, they could not be reclaimed under the extradition treaty. The fact that Thompson and other rebel agents held blank commissions, as I have said, has been proved, and a copy of one of them is of record here.

This witness also testifies to a conversation with William C. Cleary, shortly after the surrender of Lee's army, and on the day before the President's assassination, at the St. Lawrence hotel, Montreal, when speaking of the rejoicing in the States over the capture of Richmond, Cleary said; "they would put the laugh on the other side of their mouth *in a day or two.*" These parties knew that Conover was in the secret of the assassination, and talked with him about it as freely as they would speak of the weather. Before the assassination he had a conversation also with Sanders, who asked him if he knew Booth well, and expressed some apprehension that Booth would "make a failure of it; that he was desperate and reckless, and he was afraid the whole thing would prove a failure."

Dr. James D. Merritt testifies that George Young, one of the parties named in the record, declared in his presence, in Canada, last fall, that Lincoln should never be inaugurated; that they had friends in Washington, who, I suppose, were some of the same friends referred to in the despatch of October 13, and which Davis had directed them "to set to work." George N. Sanders also said to him "that Lincoln would keep himself mighty close if he did serve another term;" while Steele and other confederates declared that the tyrant never should serve another term. He heard the assassination discussed at a meeting of these rebel agents in Montreal in February last. "Sanders said they had *plenty of money* to accomplish the assassination, and named over a number of persons who were ready and willing to engage in undertaking to remove the President, Vice President, the cabinet, and some of the leading generals. At this meeting he read a letter which he had received from Davis, which justified him in making any arrangements that he could to accomplish the object." This letter the witness heard read, and it, in substance, declared that if the people in Canada and the southerners in the States were willing to submit to be governed by such a tyrant as Lincoln, he didn't wish to recognize them as friends. The letter was read openly; it was also handed to Colonel Steele, George Young, Hill, and Scott, to be read. This was about the middle of February last. At this meeting Sanders named over the persons who were willing to accomplish the assassination, and among the persons thus named was Booth, whom the witness had seen in Canada in October;

5 B

also George Harper, one of the conspirators named on the record, Caldwell, Randall, Harrison, and Surratt.

The witness understood, from the reading of the letter, that if the President, Vice-President, and cabinet could be disposed of it would satisfy the people of the north that the southerners had *friends* in the north ; that a peace could be obtained on better terms ; that the rebels had endeavored to bring about a war between the United States and England, and that Mr. Seward, through his energy and sagacity, had thwarted all their efforts; that was given as a reason for removing him. On the 5th or 6th of last April this witness met George Harper, Caldwell, Randall, and others, who are spoken of in this meeting at Montreal as engaged to assassinate the President and cabinet, when Harper said they were going to the States to make a row such as had never been heard of, and added that "if I (the witness) did not hear of the death of Old Abe, of the Vice-President, and of General Dix in less than ten days, I might put him down as a fool. That was on the 6th of April. He mentioned that Booth was in Washington at that time. He said they had plenty of friends in Washington, and that some fifteen or twenty were going."

This witness ascertained, on the 8th of April, that Harper and others had left for the States. The proof is that these parties could come through to Washington from Montreal or Toronto in thirty-six hours. They did come, and within the ten days named by Harper the President was murdered ! Some attempts have been made to discredit this witness, (Dr. Merritt,) not by the examination of witnesses in court, not by any apparent want of truth in the testimony. but by the *ex parte* statements of these rebel agents in Canada and their hired advocates in the United States. There is a statement upon the record, verified by an official communication from the War Department, which shows the truthfulness of this witness, and that is, that before the assassination, learning that Harper and his associates had started for the States, informed as he was of their purpose to assassinate the President, cabinet, and leading generals, Merritt deemed it his duty to call, and did call, on the 10th of April, upon a justice of the peace in Canada, named Davidson, and gave him the information, that he might take steps to stop these proceedings. The correspondence on this subject with Davidson has been brought into court. Dr. Merritt testifies, further, that after this meeting in Montreal he had a conversation with Clement C. Clay, in Toronto, about the letter from Jefferson Davis which Sanders had exhibited, in which conversation Clay gave the witness to understand that he knew the nature of the letter perfectly, and remarked that he thought "the end would justify the means." The witness also testifies to the presence of Booth with Sanders in Montreal last fall, and of Surratt in Toronto in February last.

The court must be satisfied, by the manner of this and other witnesses to the transactions in Canada, as well as by the fact that they are wholly uncontradicted in any material matter that they state, that they speak the truth, and that the several parties named on your record, Davis, Thompson, Cleary, Tucker, Clay, Young, Harper, Booth, and John H. Surratt did combine and conspire together in Canada to kill and murder Abraham Lincoln, Andrew Johnson, William H. Seward, and Ulysses S. Grant. That this agreement was substantially entered into by Booth and the agents of Davis in Canada as early as October there cannot be any doubt. The language of Thompson at that time and before was, that he was in favor of the assassination. His further language was, that he knew the men who were ready to do it; and Booth, it is shown, was there at that time, and, as Thompson's secretary says, was one of the men referred to by Thompson.

The fact that others, besides the parties named on the record, were, by the terms of the conspiracy, to be assassinated, in nowise affects the case now on trial. If it is true that these parties did conspire to murder other parties, as well as those named upon the record, the substance of the charge is proved.

It is also true that if, in pursuance of that conspiracy, Booth, confederated with Surratt and the accused, killed and murdered Abraham Lincoln, the charge and specification is proved literally as stated on your record, although their conspiracy embraced other persons. In law the case stands, though it may appear that the conspiracy was to kill and murder the parties named in the record and others not named in the record. If the proof is that the accused, with Booth, Surratt, Davis, &c., conspired to kill and murder one or more of the persons named, the charge of conspiracy is proved.

The declaration of Sanders, as proved, that there was plenty of money to carry out this assassination, is very strongly corroborated by the testimony of Mr. Campbell, cashier of the Ontario Bank, who states that Thompson, during the current year preceding the assassination, had upon deposit in the Montreal branch of the Ontario Bank six hundred and forty-nine thousand dollars, besides large sums to his credit in other banks in the province.

There is a further corroboration of the testimony of Conover as to the meeting of Thompson and Surratt in Montreal, and the delivery of the despatches from Richmond, on the 6th or 7th of April, first, in the fact which is shown by the testimony of Chester, that in the winter or spring Booth said he himself or some other party must go to Richmond, and, second, by the letter of Arnold dated 27th of March last, that he preferred Booth's first query, that he would first go to Richmond and see how they would take it, manifestly alluding to the proposed assassination of the President. It does not follow because Davis had written a letter in February which, in substance, approved the general object, that the parties were fully satisfied with it; because it is clear there was to be some arrangement made about the funds; and it is also clear that Davis had not before as distinctly approved and sanctioned this act as his agents either in Canada or here desired. Booth said to Chester, "We must have money; there is money in this business, and if you will enter into it I will place three thousand dollars at the disposal of your family; but I have no money myself, and must go to Richmond," or one of the parties must go, "to get money to carry out the enterprise." This was one of the arrangements that was to be "made right in Canada." The funds at Thompson's disposal, as the banker testifies, were exclusively raised by drafts of the secretary of the treasury of the Confederate States upon London, deposited in their bank to the credit of Thompson.

Accordingly, about the 27th of March, Surratt did go to Richmond. On the 3d of April he returned to Washington, and the same day left for Canada. Before leaving, he stated to Weichmann that when in Richmond he had had a conversation with Davis and with Benjamin. The fact in this connexion is not to be overlooked, that on or about the day Surratt arrived in Montreal, April 6, Jacob Thompson, as the cashier of the Ontario Bank states, drew of these confederate funds the sum of one hundred and eighty thousand dollars in the form of certificates, which, as the bank officer testifies, "might be used anywhere."

What more is wanting? Surely no word further need be spoken to show that John Wilkes Booth was in this conspiracy; that John H. Surratt was in this conspiracy; and that Jefferson Davis and his several agents named, in Canada, were in this conspiracy. If any additional evidence is wanting to show the complicity of Davis in it, let the paper found in the possession of his hired assassin Booth come to bear witness against him. That paper contained the secret cipher which Davis used in his state department at Richmond, which he employed in communicating with his agents in Canada, and which they employed in the letter of October 13, notifying him that "their friends would be set to work as *he had directed.*" The letter in cipher found in Booth's possession is translated here by the use of the cipher machine now in court, which, as the testimony of Mr. Dana shows, he brought from the rooms of Davis's state department in Richmond. Who gave Booth this secret cipher? Of what use was it to him if he was not in confederation with Davis?

But there is one other item of testimony that ought, among honest and intelligent people at all conversant with this evidence, to end all further inquiry as to whether Jefferson Davis was one of the parties, with Booth, as charged upon this record, in the conspiracy to assassinate the President and others. That is, that on the fifth day after the assassination, in the city of Charlotte, North Carolina, a telegraphic despatch was received by him, at the house of Mr. Bates, from John C. Breckinridge, his rebel secretary of war, which despatch is produced here, identified by the telegraph agent, and placed upon your record in the words following:

"GREENSBORO', *April* 19, 1865.
"*His Excellency President Davis :*

"President Lincoln was assassinated in the theatre in Washington on the night of the 14th inst. Seward's house was entered on the same night and he was repeatedly stabbed, and is probably mortally wounded.
"JOHN C. BRECKINRIDGE."

At the time this despatch was handed to him, Davis was addressing a meeting from the steps of Mr. Bates's house, and after reading the despatch to the people he said: "If it were to be done, it were *better* it were well done." Shortly afterwards, in the house of the witness, in the same city, Breckinridge, having come to see Davis, stated his regret that the occurrence had happened, because he deemed it unfortunate for the people of the south at that time. Davis replied, referring to the assassination, "Well, general, I don't know; if it were to be done at all, it were *better* that it were well done ; and if the same had been done to Andy Johnson, the beast, and to Secretary Stanton, the job would then be *complete.*"

Accomplished as this man was in all the arts of a conspirator, he was not equal to the task—as happily, in the good providence of God, no mortal man is—of concealing, by any form of words, any great crime which he may have meditated or perpetrated either against his government or his fellow-men. It was doubtless furthest from

Jefferson Davis's purpose to make confession, and yet he did make a confession. His guilt demanded utterance; that demand he could not resist; therefore his words proclaimed his guilt, in spite of his purpose to conceal it. He said, "if it were to be done, it were *better* it were *well done.*" Would any man ignorant of the conspiracy be able to devise and fashion such a form of speech as that? Had not the President been murdered? Had he not reason to believe that the Secretary of State had been mortally wounded? Yet he was not satisfied, but was compelled to say, "it were *better* it were *well done*"—that is to say, all that had been agreed to be done had not been done. Two days afterwards, in his conversation with Breckinridge, he not only repeats the same form of expression, "if it were to be done it were *better* it were *well done,*" but adds these words: "And if the same had been done to Andy Johnson, the beast, and to Secretary Stanton, the *job* would *then be complete.*" He would accept the assassination of the President, the Vice President, of the Secretary of State and the Secretary of War, as a complete execution of the "job," which he had given out upon contract, and which he had "made all right," so far as the pay was concerned, by the despatches he had sent to Thompson by Surratt, one of his hired assassins. Whatever may be the conviction of others, my own conviction is that Jefferson Davis is as clearly proven guilty of this conspiracy as is John Wilkes Booth, by whose hand Jefferson Davis inflicted the mortal wound upon Abraham Lincoln. His words of intense hate, and rage, and disappointment are not to be overlooked—that the assassins had not done their work *well*; that they had not succeeded in robbing the people altogether of their constitutional Executive and his advisers; and hence he exclaims, "If they had killed Andy Johnson, the beast!" Neither can he conceal his chagrin and disappointment that the War Minister of the republic, whose energy, incorruptible integrity, sleepless vigilance, and executive ability had organized day by day, month by month, and year by year, victory for our arms, had escaped the knife of the hired assassins. The job, says this procurer of assassination, was not well done; it had been *better* if it had been well done! Because Abraham Lincoln had been clear in his great office, and had saved the nation's life by enforcing the nation's laws, this traitor declares he must be murdered; because Mr. Seward, as the foreign secretary of the country, had thwarted the purposes of treason to plunge his country into a war with England, he must be murdered; because, upon the murder of Mr. Lincoln, Andrew Johnson would succeed to the presidency, and because he had been true to the Constitution and government, faithful found among the faithless of his own State, clinging to the falling pillars of the republic when others had fled, he must be murdered; and because the Secretary of War had taken care, by the faithful discharge of his duties, that the republic should live and not die, he must be murdered. Inasmuch as these two faithful officers were not also assassinated, assuming that the Secretary of State was mortally wounded, Davis could not conceal his disappointment and chagrin that the work was not "well done," that "the job was not complete!"

Thus it appears by the testimony that the proposition made to Davis was to kill and murder the deadliest enemies of the confederacy—not to kidnap them, as is now pretended here ; that by the declaration of Sanders, Tucker, Thompson, Clay, Cleary, Harper and Young, the conspirators in Canada, the agreement and combination among them was to kill and murder Abraham Lincoln, William H. Seward, Andrew Johnson, Ulysses S. Grant, Edwin M. Stanton, and others of his advisors, and not to kidnap them ; it appears from every utterance of John Wilkes Booth, as well as from the Charles Selby letter, of which mention will presently be made, that, as early as November, the proposition with him was to kill and murder, not to kidnap.

Since the first examination of Conover, who testified, as the court will remember, to many important facts against these conspirators and agents of Davis in Canada—among others, the terrible and fiendish plot disclosed by Thompson, Pallen, and others, that they had ascertained the volume of water in the reservoir supplying New York city, estimated the quantity of poison required to render it deadly, and intended thus to poison a whole city—Conover returned to Canada, by direction of this court, for the purpose of obtaining certain documentary evidence. There, about the 9th of June, he met Beverley Tucker, Sanders, and other conspirators, and conversed with them. Tucker declared that Secretary Stanton, whom he denounced as "a scoundrel," and Judge Holt, whom he called "a bloodthirsty villain," "could protect themselves as long as they remained in office by a guard, but that would not always be the case, and, by the Eternal, he had a large account to settle with them." After this, the evidence of Conover here having been published, these parties called upon him and asked him whether he had been to Washington, and had testified before this court. Conover denied it ; they insisted, and took him to a room, where, with drawn pistols, they compelled him to consent to make an affidavit that he had been falsely personated here by another, and that he would make that affidavit before a

Mr. Kerr, who would witness it. They then called in Mr. Kerr to certify to the public that Conover had made such a denial. They also compelled this witness to furnish for publication an advertisement offering a reward of five hundred dollars for the arrest of the "infamous and perjured scoundrel" who had recently personated James W. Wallace under the name of Sanford Conover, and testified to a tissue of falsehoods before the military commission at Washington, which advertisement was published in the papers.

To these facts Mr. Conover now testifies, and also discloses the fact that these same men published, in the report of the proceedings before Judge Smith, an affidavit purporting to be his, but which he never made. The affidavit which he in fact made, and which was published in a newspaper at that time, produced here, is set out substantially upon your record, and agrees with the testimony upon the same point given by him in this court.

To suppose that Conover ever made such an affidavit voluntarily as the one wrung from him as stated is impossible. Would he advertise for his own arrest and charge himself with falsely personating himself? But the fact cannot evade observation, that when these guilty conspirators saw Conover's testimony before this court in the public prints, revealing to the world the atrocious plots of these felon conspirators, conscious of the truthfulness of his statements, they cast about at once for some defence before the public, and devised the foolish and stupid invention of compelling him to make an affidavit that he was not Sanford Conover, was not in this court, never gave this testimony, but was a practicing lawyer in Montreal! This infamous proceeding, coupled with the evidence before detailed, stamps these ruffian plotters with the guilt of this conspiracy.

John Wilkes Booth having entered into this conspiracy in Canada, as has been shown, as early as October, he is next found in the city of New York on the 11th day, as I claim, of November, in disguise, in conversation with another, the conversation disclosing to the witness, Mrs. Hudspeth, that they had some matter of personal interest between them; that upon one of them the lot had fallen to go to Washington—upon the other to go to Newbern. This witness, upon being shown the photograph of Booth, swears "that the face is the same" as that of one of those men, who she says was a young man of education and culture, as appeared by his conversation, and who had a scar like a bite near the jaw-bone. It is a fact proved here by the Surgeon General that Booth had such a scar on the side of his neck. Mrs. Hudspeth heard him say he would leave for Washington the day after to-morrow. His companion appeared angry because it had not fallen on him to go to Washington. This took place after the presidential election in November. She cannot fix the precise date, but says she was told that General Butler left New York on that day. The testimony discloses that General Butler's army was on the 11th of November leaving New York. The register of the National Hotel shows that Booth left Washington on the early morning train, November 11, and that he returned to this city on the 14th. Chester testifies positively to Booth's presence in New York early in November. This testimony shows most conclusively that Booth was in New York on the 11th of November. The early morning train on which he left Washington would reach New York early in the afternoon of that day. Chester saw him there early in November, and Mrs. Hudspeth not only identifies his picture, but describes his person. The scar upon his neck near his jaw was peculiar and is well described by the witness as like a bite. On that day Booth had a letter in his possession which he accidentally dropped in the street car in the presence of Mrs. Hudspeth, the witness, who delivered it to Major General Dix the same day, and by whom, as his letter on file before this court shows, the same was transmitted to the War Department November 17, 1864. That letter contains these words:

"DEAR LOUIS: The time has at last come that we have all so wished for, and upon you everything depends. As it was decided, before you left, we were to cast lots, we accordingly did so, and you are to be the Charlotte Corday of the 19th century. When you remember the fearful, solemn vow that was taken by us, you will feel there is no drawback. *Abe* must *die*, and *now*. You can choose your weapons— *the cup, the knife, the bullet*. The cup failed us once, and might again. Johnson, who will give *this*, has been like an enraged demon since the meeting, because it has not fallen upon him to rid the world of the monster. * * * You know where *to find your friends*. Your *disguises* are so perfect and complete that without *one* knew your *face*, no police telegraphic despatch would catch you. The English gentleman, *Harcourt*, must not act hastily. Remember he has ten days. *Strike for your home, strike for your country; bide your time, but strike sure*. Get introduced; congratulate him; listen to his stories; (not many more will the brute tell to earthly friends;) do anything but fail, and meet us at the appointed place within the fortnight. You will probably hear from me in Washington. Sanders is doing us no good in Canada.

"CHAS. SELBY."

The learned gentleman, (Mr. Cox,) in his very able and carefully considered argument in defence of O'Laughlin and Arnold, attached importance to this letter, and doubtless very clearly saw its bearing upon the case, and therefore undertook to show that the witness, Mrs. Hudspeth, must be mistaken as to the person of Booth. The gentleman assumes that the letter of General Dix, of the 17th of November last, transmitting this letter to the War Department, reads that the party who dropped the letter was heard to say that he would start to Washington on Friday night next, although the word "next" is not in the letter, neither is it in the quotation which the gentleman makes, for he quotes it fairly; yet he concludes that this would be the 18th of November.

Now the fact is, the 11th of November last was Friday, and the register of the National Hotel bears witness that Mrs. Hudspeth is not mistaken; because her language is, that Booth said he would leave for Washington day after to-morrow, which would be Sunday, the 13th, and if in the evening, would bring him to Washington on Monday, the 14th of November, the day on which, the register shows, he did return to the National Hotel. As to the improbability which the gentleman raises, on the conversation happening in a street car, crowded with people, there was nothing that transpired, although the conversation was earnest, which enabled the witness, or could have enabled any one, in the absence of this letter, or of the subsequent conduct of Booth, to form the least idea of the subject-matter of their conversation. The gentleman does not deal altogether fairly in his remarks touching the letter of General Dix; because, upon a careful examination of the letter, it will be found that he did not form any such judgment as that it was a hoax for the Sunday Mercury, but he took care to forward it to the Department, and asked attention to it; when, as appears by the testimony of the Assistant Secretary of War, Mr. Dana, the letter was delivered to Mr. Lincoln, who considered it important enough to indorse it with the word "Assassination," and file it in his office, where it was found after the commission of this crime, and brought into this court to bear witness against his assassins.

Although this letter would imply that the assassination spoken of was to take place speedily, yet the party was *to bide his time.* Though he had entered into the preliminary arrangements in Canada, although conspirators had doubtless agreed to co-operate with him in the commission of the crime, and lots had been cast for the chief part in the bloody drama, yet it remained for him, as the leader and principal of the hired assassins, by whose hand their employers were to strike the murderous blow, to collect about him and bring to Washington such persons as would be willing to lend themselves for a price to the horrid crime and likely to give the necessary aid and support in its consummation. The letter declares that Abraham Lincoln must die, and *now*, meaning as soon as the agents can be employed and the work done. To that end you will bide *your time*. But, says the gentleman, it could not have been the same conspiracy charged here to which this letter refers. Why not? It is charged here that Booth with the accused and others conspired to kill and murder Abraham Lincoln—that is precisely the conspiracy disclosed in the letter. Granted that the parties on trial had not then entered into the combination; if they at any time afterward entered into it they became parties to it, and the conspiracy was still the same. But, says the gentleman, the words of the letter imply that the conspiracy was to be executed within the fortnight. Booth is directed, by the name of Louis, to meet the writer within the fortnight. It by no means follows that he was to strike within the fortnight, because he was to meet his co-conspirator within that time, and any such conclusion is excluded by the words "Bide your time." Even if the conspiracy was to be executed within the fortnight, and was not so executed, and the same party, Booth, afterwards by concert and agreement with the accused and others did execute it by "striking sure" and killing the President, that act, whenever done, would be but the execution of the same conspiracy. The letter is conclusive evidence of so much of this conspiracy as relates to the murder of President Lincoln. As Booth was to do anything but fail, he immediately thereafter sought out the agents to enable him to strike sure, and execute all that he had agreed with Davis and his co-confederates in Canada to do—to murder the President, the Secretary of State, the Vice President, General Grant, and Secretary Stanton.

Even Booth's co-conspirator, Payne, now on his trial, by his defence admits all this, and says Booth had just been to Canada, "was filled with a mighty scheme, and was lying in wait for agents." Booth asked the co-operation of the prisoner Payne, and said: "I will give you as much money as you want; but first you must swear to stick by me. It is in the oil business." This you are told by the accused was early in March last. Thus guilt bears witness against itself.

We find Booth in New York in November, December, and January, urging Chester to enter into this combination, assuring him that there was *money* in it; that they had "friends on the other side;" that if he would only participate in it he would never want for money while he lived, and all that was asked of him was to stand at and open *the back door of Ford's theatre.* Booth, in his interviews with Chester, confesses that *he is without money himself*, and allows Chester to reimburse him the $50 which he (Booth) had transmitted to him in a letter for the purpose of paying his expenses to Washington as one of the parties to this conspiracy. Booth told him, although he himself was penniless, "*there is money in this*—we have friends on the other side;" and if you will but engage, I will have three thousand dollars deposited at once for the use of your family.

Failing to secure the services of Chester, because his soul recoiled with abhorrence from the foul work of assassination and murder, he found more willing instruments in others whom he gathered about him. Men to commit the assassinations, horses to secure speedy and certain escape, were to be provided, and to this end Booth, with an energy worthy of a better cause, applies himself. For this latter purpose he told Chester he had already expended $5,000. In the latter part of November, 1864, he visits Charles county, Maryland, and is in company with one of the prisoners, Dr. Samuel A. Mudd, with whom he lodged over night, and through whom he procures of Gardner one of the several horses which were at his disposal, and used by him and his co-conspirators in Washington on the night of the assassination.

Some time in January last, it is in testimony, that the prisoner Mudd introduced Booth to John H. Surratt and the witness Weichmann; that Booth invited them to the National Hotel; that when there, in the room to which Booth took them, Mudd went out into the passage, called Booth out and had a private conversation with him, leaving the witness and Surratt in the room. Upon their return to the room Booth went out with Surratt, and upon their coming in all three, Booth, Surratt, and Samuel A. Mudd, went out together and had a conversation in the passage, leaving the witness alone. Up to the time of this interview it seems that neither the witness nor Surratt had any knowledge of Booth, as they were then introduced to him by Dr. Mudd. Whether Surratt had in fact previously known Booth it is not important to inquire. Mudd deemed it necessary, perhaps a wise precaution, to introduce Surratt to Booth; he also deemed it necessary to have a private conversation with Booth shortly afterwards, and directly upon that to have a conversation together with Booth and Surratt alone. Had this conversation, no part of which was heard by the witness, been perfectly innocent, it is not to be presumed that Dr. Mudd, who was an entire stranger to Weichmann, would have deemed it necessary to hold the conversation secretly, nor to have volunteered to tell the witness, or rather pretend to tell him, what the conversation was ; yet he did say to the witness, upon their return to the room, by way of apology, I suppose, for the privacy of the conversation, that Booth had some private business with him, and wished to purchase his farm. This silly device, as is often the case in attempts at deception, failed in the execution ; for it remains to be shown how the fact that Mudd had private business with Booth, and that Booth wished to purchase his farm, made it at all necessary or even proper that they should both volunteer to call out Surratt, who up to that moment was a stranger to Booth. What had Surratt to do with Booth's purchase of Mudd's farm? And if it was necessary to withdraw and talk by themselves secretly about the sale of the farm, why should they disclose the fact to the very man from whom they had concealed it?

Upon the return of these three parties to the room, they seated themselves at a table, and upon the back of an envelope Booth traced lines with a pencil, indicating, as the witness states, the direction of roads. Why was this done? As Booth had been previously in that section of country, as the prisoner in his defence has taken great pains to show, it was certainly not necessary to anything connected with the purchase of Mudd's farm that at that time he should be indicating the direction of roads to or from it; nor is it made to appear, by anything in this testimony, how it comes that Surratt, as the witness testifies, seemed to be as much interested in the marking out of these roads as Mudd or Booth. It does not appear that Surratt was in anywise connected with or interested in the sale of Mudd's farm. From all that has transpired since this meeting at the hotel, it would seem that this plotting the roads was intended, not so much to show the road to Mudd's farm, as to point out the shortest and safest route for flight from the capital, by the houses of all the parties to this conspiracy, to their "friends on the other side."

But, says the learned gentleman, (Mr. Ewing,) in his very able argument in defence of this prisoner, why should Booth determine that his flight should be through Charles county? The answer must be obvious, upon a moment's reflection, to every man, and could not possibly have escaped the notice of the counsel himself, but for the reason that his zeal for his client constrained him to overlook it. It was absolutely essential that this murderer should have his co-conspirators at convenient points along his route, and it does not appear in evidence that by the route to his friends, who had then fled from

Richmond, which the gentleman (Mr. Ewing) indicates as the more direct, but of which there is not the slightest evidence whatever, Booth had co-conspirators at an equal distance from Washington. The testimony discloses, further, that on the route selected by him for his flight there is a large population that would be most likely to favor and aid him in the execution of his wicked purpose, and in making his escape. But it is a sufficient answer to the gentleman's question, that Booth's co-conspirator Mudd lived in Charles county.

To return to the meeting at the hotel. In the light of other facts in this case, it must become clear to the court that this secret meeting between Booth, Surratt, and Mudd was a conference looking to the execution of this conspiracy. It so impressed the prisoner—it so impressed his counsel, that they deemed it necessary and absolutely essential to their defence to attempt to destroy the credibility of the witness Weichmann.

I may say here, in passing, that they have not attempted to impeach his general reputation for truth by the testimony of a single witness, nor have they impeached his testimony by calling a single witness to discredit one material fact to which he has testified in this issue. Failing to find a breath of suspicion against Weichmann's character, or to contradict a single fact to which he testified, the accused had to fly to the last resort, an *alibi*, and very earnestly did the learned counsel devote himself to the task.

It is not material whether this meeting in the hotel took place on the 23d of December or in January. But, says the counsel, it was after the commencement or close of the Congressional holiday. That is not material; but the concurrent resolution of Congress shows that the holiday commenced on the 22d December, the day before the accused spent the evening in Washington. The witness is not certain about the date of this meeting. The material fact is, did this meeting take place—either on the 23d of December or in January last? Were the private interviews there held, and was the apology made, as detailed, by Mudd and Booth, after the secret conference, to the witness? That the meeting did take place, and that Mudd did explain that these secret interviews, with Booth first, and with Booth and Surratt directly afterward, had relation to the sale of his farm, is confessedly admitted by the endeavor of the prisoner, through his counsel, to show that negotiations had been going on between Booth and Mudd for the sale of Mudd's farm. If no such meeting was held, if no such explanation was made by Mudd to Weichmann, can any man for a moment believe that a witness would have been called here to give any testimony about Booth having negotiated for Mudd's farm? What conceivable connexion has it with this case, except to show that Mudd's explanation to Weichmann for his extraordinary conduct was in exact accordance with the fact? Or was this testimony about the negotiations for Mudd's farm intended to show so close an intimacy and intercourse with Booth that Mudd could not fail to recognize him when he came flying for aid to his house from the work of assassination? It would be injustice to the able counsel to suppose that.

I have said that it was wholly immaterial whether this conversation took place on the 23d of December or in January; it is in evidence that in both those months Booth was at the National Hotel; that he occupied a room there; that he arrived there on the 22d and was there on the 23d of December last, and also on the 12th day of January. The testimony of the witness is, that Booth said he had just come in. Suppose this conversation took place in December, on the evening of the 23d, the time when it is proved by J. T. Mudd, the witness for the accused, that he, in company with Samuel A. Mudd, spent the night in Washington city. Is there anything in the testimony of that or any other witness, to show that the accused did not have and could not have had an interview with Booth on that evening? J. T. Mudd testifies that he separated from the prisoner, Samuel A. Mudd, at the National Hotel early in the evening of that day, and did not meet him again until the accused came in for the night at the Pennsylvania House, where he stopped. Where was Dr. Samuel A. Mudd during this interval? What does his witness know about him during that time? How can he say that Dr. Mudd did not go up on Seventh street in company with Booth, then at the National; that he did not on Seventh street meet Surratt and Weichmann; that he did not return to the National Hotel; that he did not have this interview, and afterwards meet him, the witness, as he testifies, at the Pennsylvania House? Who knows that the Congressional holiday had not in fact commenced on that day? What witness has been called to prove that Booth did not on either of those occasions occupy the room that had formerly been occupied by a member of Congress, who had temporarily vacated it, leaving his books there? Weichmann, I repeat, is not positive as to the date, he is only positive as to the fact; and he disclosed voluntarily, to this court, that the date could probably be fixed by a reference to the register of the Pennsylvania House; that register cannot, of course, be conclusive of whether Mudd was there in January or not, for the very good reason that the proprietor admits that he did not know Samuel A. Mudd, therefore Mudd might have registered by any other name. Weichmann does not pretend to know that Mudd had registered at all. If Mudd was here in January, as a party to this conspiracy, it is not at all unlikely that, if he did register at that time in the presence of a man to whom he was wholly unknown, his kinsman not then being with him, he would register by a false name. But if the interview took place in December, the testimony of Weichmann bears as strongly against the accused as if it had happened in January. Weichmann says he does not know what time was occupied in this interview at the National Hotel; that it probably lasted twenty minutes; that, after the private interviews between Mudd and Surratt and Booth, which were not of very long duration, had terminated, the parties went to the Pennsylvania House, where Dr. Mudd had rooms, and after sitting together in the common sitting-room of the hotel, they left Dr. Mudd there about 10 o'clock p. m., who remained during the night. Weichmann's testimony leaves no doubt that this meeting on Seventh street and interview at the National took place after dark, and terminated before or about 10 o'clock p. m. His own witness, J. T. Mudd, after stating that he separated from the accused at the National Hotel, says after he had got through a conversation with a gentleman of his acquaintance, he walked down the Avenue, went to several clothing stores, and "after a while" walked round to the Pennsylvania House, and "very soon after" he got there Dr. Mudd came in, and they went to bed shortly afterwards. What time he spent in his "walk alone" on the Avenue, looking at clothing; what period he embraces in the terms "after a while," when he returned to the Pennsylvania House, and "soon after" which Dr. Mudd got there, the witness does not disclose. Neither does he intimate, much less testify, that he saw Dr. Mudd when he first entered the Pennsylvania House on that night after their separation. How does he know that Booth and Surrat and Weichmann did not accompany Samuel A. Mudd to that house that evening? How does he know that the prisoner and those persons did not converse together some time in the sitting-room of the Pennsylvania Hotel? Jeremiah Mudd has not testified that he met Doctor Mudd in that room, or that he was in it himself. He has, however, sworn to the fact, which is disproved by no one, that the prisoner was separated from him long enough that evening to have had the meeting with Booth, Surratt, and Weichmann, and the interviews in the National Hotel, and at the Pennsylvania House, to wnich Weichmann has testified? Who is there to disprove it? Of what importance is it whether it was on the 23d day of December or in January? How does that affect the credibility of Weichmann? He is a man, as I have before said, against whose reputation for truth and good conduct they have not been able to bring one witness. If this meeting did by possibility take place that night, is there anything to render it improbable that Booth, and Mudd, and Surratt did have the conversation at the National Hotel to which Weichmann testifies? Of what avail, therefore, is the attempt to prove that Mudd was not here during January, if it was clear that he was here on the 23d of December, 1864, and had this conversation with Booth? That this attempt to prove an *alibi* during January has failed, is quite as clear as is the proof of the fact that the prisoner was here on the evening of the 23d of December, and present in the National Hotel, where Booth stopped. The fact that the prisoner, Samuel A. Mudd, went with J. T. Mudd on that evening to the National Hotel, and there separated from him, is proved by his own witness, J. T. Mudd; and that he did not rejoin him until they retired to bed in the Pennsylvania House is proved by the same witness, and contradicted by nobody. Does any one suppose there would have been such assiduous care to prove that the prisoner was with his kinsman all the time on the 23d of December in Washington, if they had not known that Booth was then at the National Hotel, and that a meeting of the prisoner with Booth, Surratt, and Weichmann on that day would corroborate and confirm Weichmann's testimony in every material statement he made concerning that meeting?

The accused having signally failed to account for his absence after he separated from his witness, J. T. Mudd, early in the evening of the 23d of December, at the National Hotel, until they had again met at the Pennsylvania House, when they retired to rest, he now attempts to prove an *alibi* as to the month of January. In this he has failed, as he failed in the attempt to show that he could not have met Booth, Surratt, and Weichmann on the 23d of December.

For this purpose the accused calls Betty Washington. She had been at Mudd's house every night since the Monday after Christmas last, except when here at court, and says that the prisoner, Mudd, has only been away from home three nights during that time. This witness forgets that Mudd has not been at home any night or day since this court assembled. Neither does she account for the three nights in which she swears, to his absence from home. First, she says he went to Gardner's party; second, he went to Giesboro, then to Washington. She does not know in what month he was away, the second time, all night. She only knows where he went, from what he and his wife said, which is not evidence; but she does testify that when he left home and was absent over night, the second time, it was about two or three weeks after she came to his house, which would, if it were three weeks, make it just about the 15th of January, 1865; because she swears she came to his house on the first Monday after Christmas last, which was the 26th day of December; so that the 15th of January would be three weeks, less one day, from that time; and it might have been a week earlier according to her testimony, as, also, it might have been a week earlier, or more, by Weichmann's testimony, for he is not positive as to the time. What I have said of the register of the Pennsylvania House, the headquarters of Mudd and Atzerodt, I need not here repeat. That record proves nothing, save that Dr. Mudd was there on the 23d of December, which, as we have seen, is a fact, along with others, to show that the meeting at the National then took place. I have also called the attention of the court to the fact that if Mudd was at that house again in January, and did not register his name, that fact proves nothing; or, if he did, the register only proves that he registered falsely; either of which facts might have happened without the knowledge of the witness called by the accused from that house, who does not know Samuel A. Mudd personally.

The testimony of Henry L. Mudd, his brother, in support of this *alibi*, is, that the prisoner was in Washington on the 23d of March, and on the 10th of April, four days before the murder! But he does not account for the absent night in January, about which Betty Washington testifies. Thomas Davis was called for the same purpose, but stated that he was himself absent one night in January, after the 9th of that month, and he could not say whether Mudd was there on that night or not. He does testify to Mudd's absence over night three times, and fixes one occasion on the night of the 26th of January. In consequence of his own absence one night in January, this witness cannot account for the absence of Mudd on the night referred to by Betty Washington.

This matter is entitled to no further attention. It can satisfy no one, and the burden of proof is upon the prisoner to prove that he was not in Washington in January last. How can such testimony convince any rational man that Mudd was not here in January, against the evidence of an unimpeached witness, who swears that Samuel A.

Mudd was in Washington in the month of January? Who that has been examined here as a witness knows that he was not?

The Rev. Mr. Evans swears that he saw him in Washington last winter, and that at the same time he saw Jarboe, the one coming out of, and the other going into, a house on H street, which he was informed on inquiry was the house of Mrs. Surratt. Jarboe is the only witness called to contradict Mr. Evans, and he leaves it in extreme doubt whether he does not corroborate him, as he swears that he was here himself last winter or fall, but cannot state exactly the time. Jarboe's silence on questions touching his own credibility leaves no room for any one to say that his testimony could impeach Mr. Evans, whatever he might swear.

Miss Anna H. Surratt is also called for the purpose of impeaching Mr. Evans. It is sufficient to say of her testimony on that point that she swears negatively only—that she did not see either of the persons named at her mother's house. This testimony neither disproves, nor does it even tend to disprove, the fact put in issue by Mr. Evans. No one will pretend, whatever the form of her expression in giving her testimony, that she could say more than that she did not know the fact, as it was impossible that she could know who was, or who was not, at her mother's house, casually, at a period so remote. It is not my purpose, neither is it needful here, to question in any way the integrity of this young woman.

It is further in testimony that Samuel A. Mudd was here on the 3d day of March last, the day preceding the inauguration, when Booth was to strike the traitorous blow; and it was, doubtless, only by the interposition of that God who stands within the shadow and keeps watch above his own, that the victim of this conspiracy was spared that day from the assassin's hand that he might complete his work and see the salvation of his country in the fall of Richmond and the surrender of its great army. Dr. Mudd was here on that day (the 3d of March) to abet, to encourage, to nerve his co-conspirator for the commission of this great crime. He was carried away by the awful purpose which possessed him, and rushed into the room of Mr. Norton at the National Hotel in search of Booth, exclaiming excitedly: "I'm mistaken; I thought this was Mr. Booth's room." He is told Mr. Booth is above, on the next floor. He is followed by Mr. Norton, because of his rude and excited behavior, and being followed, conscious of his guilty errand, he turns away, afraid of himself and afraid to be found in concert with his fellow confederate.

Mr. Norton identifies the prisoner, and has no doubt that Samuel A. Mudd is the man.

The Rev. Mr. Evans also swears that, after the 1st and before the 4th day of March last, he is certain that within that time, and on the 2d or 3d of March, he saw Dr. Mudd drive into Washington city. The endeavor is made by the accused, in order to break down this witness, by proving another *alibi*. The sister of the accused, Miss Fanny Mudd, is called. She testifies that she saw the prisoner at breakfast in her father's house, on the 2d of March, about 5 o'clock in the morning, and not again until the 3d of March at noon. Mrs. Emily Mudd swears substantially to the same statement. Betty Washington, called for the accused, swears that he was at home all day at work with her on the 2d of March, and took breakfast at home. Frank Washington swears that Mudd was at home all day; that he saw him when he first came out in the morning about sunrise from his own house, and knows that he was there all day with them. Which is correct, the testimony of his sisters or the testimony of his servants? The sisters say that he was at their father's house for breakfast on the morning of the 2d of March; the servants say he was at home for breakfast with them on that day. If this testimony is followed, it proves one *alibi* too much. It is impossible, in the nature of things, that the testimony of all these four witnesses can be true.

Seeing this weakness in the testimony brought to prove this second *alibi*, the endeavor is next made to discredit Mr. Norton for truth; and two witnesses, not more, are called, who testify that his reputation for truth has suffered by contested litigation between one of the impeaching witnesses and others. Four witnesses are called, who testify that Mr. Norton's reputation for truth is very good; that he is a man of high character for truth, and entitled to be believed whether he speaks under the obligation of an oath or not. The late Postmaster General, Hon. Horatio King, not only sustains Mr. Norton as a man of good reputation for truth, but expressly corroborates his testimony, by stating that in March last, about the 4th of March, Mr. Norton told him the same fact to which he swears here: that a man came into his room under excitement, alarmed his sister, was followed out by himself, and went down stairs instead of going up; and that Mr. Norton told him this before the assassination, and about the time of the inauguration. What motive had Mr. Norton at that time to fabricate this statement? It detracts nothing from his testimony that he did not at that time mention the name of this man to his friend, Mr. King; because it appears from his testimony—and there is none to question the truthfulness of his statement—that at that time he did not know his name. Neither does it take from the force of this testimony, that Mr. Norton did not, in communicating this matter to Mr. King, make mention of Booth's name; because there was nothing in the transaction, at the time, he being ignorant of the name of Mudd, and equally ignorant of the conspiracy between Mudd and Booth, to give the least occasion for any mention of Booth or of the transaction further than as he detailed it. With such corroboration, who can doubt the fact that Mudd did enter the room of Mr. Norton, and was followed by him, on the 3d of March last? Can he be mistaken in the man? Whoever looks at the prisoner carefully once will be sure to recognize him again.

For the present I pass from the consideration of the testimony showing Dr. Mudd's connection with Booth in this conspiracy, with the remark that it is in evidence, and I think established, both by the testimony adduced by the prosecution and that by the prisoner, that since the commencement of this rebellion John H. Surratt visited the prisoner's house; that he concealed Surratt and other rebels and traitors in the woods near his house, where for several days he furnished them with food and bedding; that the shelter of the woods by night and by day was the only shelter that the prisoner dare furnish *these friends* of his; that in November Booth visited him and remained over night; that he accompanied Booth at that time to Gardner's, from whom he purchased one of the horses used on the night of the assassination to aid the escape of one of his confederates; that the prisoner had secret interviews with Booth and Surratt, as sworn to by the witness Weichmann, in the National Hotel, whether on the 23d of December or in January is a matter of entire indifference; that he rushed into Mr. Norton's room on the 3d of March in search of Booth; and that he was here again on the 10th of April, four days before the murder of the President. Of his conduct after the assassination of the President, which is confirmatory of all this—his conspiring with Booth and his sheltering, concealing, and aiding the flight of his co-conspirator, this felon assassin—I shall speak hereafter, leaving him for the present with the remark that the attempt to prove his character has resulted in showing him in sympathy with the rebellion, so cruel that he shot one of his slaves and declared his purpose to send several of them to work on the rebel batteries in Richmond.

What others, besides Samuel A. Mudd and John H. Surratt and Lewis Payne, did Booth, after his return from Canada, induce to join him in this conspiracy to murder the President, the Vice President, the Secretary of State, and the Lieutenant General, with the intent thereby to aid the rebellion and overthrow the government and laws of the United States?

On the 10th of February the prisoners Arnold and O'Laughlin came to Washington and took rooms in the house of Mrs. Vantyne; were armed; were there visited frequently by John Wilkes Booth, and alone; were occasionally absent when Booth called, who seemed anxious for their return—would sometimes leave notes for them, and sometimes a request that when they came in they should be told to come to the stable. On the 18th of March last, when Booth played in "The Apostate," the witness, Mrs. Vantyne, received from O'Laughlin complimentary tickets. These persons remained there until the 20th of March. They were visited, so far as the witness knows, during their stay at her house only by Booth, save that on a single occasion an unknown man came to see them, and remained with them over night. They told the witness they were in the "oil business." With Mudd, the guilty purpose was sought to be concealed by declaring that he was in the "land business;" with O'Laughlin and Arnold it was attempted to be concealed by the pretence that they were in the "oil business." Booth, it is proved, had closed up all connexion with oil business last September. There is not a word of testimony to show that the accused, O'Laughlin and Arnold, ever invested or sought to invest, in any way or to any amount, in the oil business; their silly words betray them; they forgot when they uttered that false statement that truth is strong, next to the Almighty, and that their crime must find them out was the irrevocable and irresistible law of nature and of nature's God.

One of their co-conspirators, known as yet only to the guilty parties to this damnable plot and to the Infinite, who will unmask and avenge all blood-guiltiness, comes to bear witness, unwittingly, against them. This unknown conspirator, who dates his letter at South Branch Bridge, April 6, 1865, mailed and postmarked Cumberland, Maryland, and addressed to John Wilkes Booth, by his initials, "J. W. B., National Hotel, Washington, D. C.," was also in the "oil speculation." In that letter he says:

"FRIEND WILKES: I received yours of March 12th, and reply as soon as practicable. I saw French, Brady, and others about the oil speculation. The subscription to the stock amounts to eight thousand dollars, and I add one thousand myself, which is about all I can stand. Now, when you sink your well, go *deep enough; don't fail;* everything depends upon you and your *helpers.*

If you cannot get through on *your trip* after you strike oil, strike through Thornton gap and across by Capon, Romney, and down the Branch. I can keep you *safe* from all hardships for a year. I am clear of all surveillance now that infernal Purdy is beat. * * * *

"I send this by Tom, and if he don't get drunk you will get it the 9th. At all events, it cannot be *understood* if lost. * * * *

"No more, only *Jake* will be at Green's *with the funds*. (Signed) LON."

That this letter is not a fabrication is made apparent by the testimony of Purdy, whose name occurs in the letter. He testified that he had been a detective in the government service, and that he had been falsely accused, as the letter recites, and put under arrest; that there was a noted rebel by the name of Green living at Thornton gap; that there was a servant, who drank, known as "Tom," in the neighborhood of South Branch Bridge; that there is an obscure route through the gap, and as described in the letter; and that a man commonly called "Lon" lives at South Branch Bridge. If the court are satisfied—and it is for them to judge—that this letter was written before the assassination, as it purports to have been, and on the day of its date, there can be no question with any one who reads it that the writer was in the conspiracy, and knew that the time of its execution drew nigh. If a conspirator, every word of its contents is evidence against every other party to this conspiracy.

Who can fail to understand this letter? His words, "go deep enough," "don't fail," "everything depends on you and your helpers," "if you can't get through on your *trip* after you *strike oil*, strike through Thornton gap," &c., and "I can keep you safe from all hardships for a year," necessarily imply that when he "*strikes oil*" there will be an occasion for *a flight*; that *a trip*, or route, has already been determined upon; that he may not be able to go through by that route; in which event he is to strike for Thornton gap, and across by Capon and Romney, and down the branch, for the shelter which his co-conspirator offers him. "I am clear of all surveillance now"—does any one doubt that the man who wrote those words wished to assure Booth that he was no longer watched, and that Booth could safely hide with him from his pursuers? Does any one doubt, from the further expression in this letter, "Jake will be at Green's with the funds," that this was a part of the price of blood, or that the eight thousand dollars subscribed by others, and the one thousand additional, subscribed by the writer, were also a part of the price to be paid?

"The oil business," which was the declared business of O'Laughlin and Arnold, was the declared business of the infamous writer of this letter; was the declared business of John H. Surratt; was the declared business of Booth himself, as explained to Chester and Payne; was "*the business*" referred to in his telegrams to O'Laughlin, and meant the murder of the President, of his cabinet, and of General Grant. The first of these telegrams is dated Washington, 13th March, and is addressed to M. O'Laughlin, No. 57 North Exeter street, Baltimore, Maryland, and is as follows: "Don't you fear to neglect your business; you had better come on at once. J. Booth." The telegraphic operator, Hoffman, who sent this despatch from Washington, swears that John Wilkes Booth delivered it to him in person on the day of its date; and the handwriting of the original telegram is established beyond question to be that of Booth. The other telegram is dated Washington, March 27, addressed "M. O'Laughlin, Esq., 57 North Exeter street, Baltimore, Maryland," and is as follows: "Get word to Sam. Come on with or without him on Wednesday morning. We sell that day sure; don't fail. J. Wilkes Booth." The original of this telegram is also proved to be in the handwriting of Booth. The sale referred to in this last telegram was doubtless the murder of the President and others—the "oil speculation," in which the writer of the letter from South Branch Bridge, dated April 6, had taken a thousand dollars, and in which Booth said there was money, and Sanders said there was money, and Atzerodt said there was money. The words of this telegram, "get word to Sam," mean Samuel Arnold, his co-conspirator, who had been with him during all his stay in Washington, at Mrs. Vantyne's. These parties to this conspiracy, after they had gone to Baltimore, had additional correspondence with Booth, which the court must infer had relation to carrying out the purposes of their confederation and agreement. The colored witness, Williams, testifies that John Wilkes Booth handed him a letter for Michael O'Laughlin, and another for Samuel Arnold, in Baltimore, some time in March last; one of which he delivered to O'Laughlin at the theatre in Baltimore, and the other to a lady at the door where Arnold boarded in Baltimore.

Their agreement and co-operation in the common object having been thus established, the letter written to Booth by the prisoner Arnold, dated March 27, 1865, the handwriting of which is proved before the court, and which was found in Booth's possession after the assassination, becomes testimony against O'Laughlin, as well as against the writer Arnold, because it is an act done in furtherance of their combination. That letter is as follows:

"DEAR JOHN: Was business so important that you could not remain in Baltimore till I saw you? I came in as soon as I could, but found you had gone to Washington. I called also to see *Mike*, but learned from his mother he had gone out with you and had not returned. I concluded, therefore, he had gone with you. How inconsiderate you have been! When I left you, you stated that *we would not meet* in a month or so, and therefore I made application for employment, an answer to which I shall receive during the week. I told my parents I had ceased with you. Can I then, under existing circumstances, act as you request? You know full well that the government suspicions something is going on there, therefore the *undertaking* is becoming more complicated. Why not, *for the present*, desist?—for various reasons, which, if you look into, you can readily see without my making any mention thereof. You nor any one can censure me for my present course. You have been its cause, for how can I now come after telling them I had left you? Suspicion rests upon me now from my whole family, and even parties in the country. I will be compelled to leave home any how, and how soon I care not. None, no, not one, were more in favor of the enterprise than myself, and to-day would be there had you not done as you have. By this, I mean manner of proceeding. I am, as you well know, in *need*. I am, you may say, in rags, whereas, to-day, I ought to be *well clothed*. I do not feel right stalking about with *means*, and more from appearances a beggar. I feel my dependence. But, even all this would have been, and was, forgotten, for I *was one with you*. Time more propitious will arrive yet. Do not act rashly or in haste. I would prefer your first query, 'Go and see how it will be taken in Richmond,' and *ere long* I shall be better prepared *to again be with you*. I dislike writing. Would sooner verbally make known my views. Yet your now waiting causes me thus to proceed. Do not in anger peruse this. Weigh all I have said, and, as a rational man and a *friend*, you cannot censure or upbraid my conduct. I sincerely trust this, nor aught else that shall or may occur, will ever be an obstacle to obliterate our former friendship and attachment. Write me to Baltimore, as I expect to be in about Wednesday or Thursday; or, if you can possibly come on, I will Tuesday meet you at Baltimore at B.

"Ever, I subscribe myself, your friend,

SAM."

Here is the confession of the prisoner Arnold, that he was one with Booth in this conspiracy; the further confession that they are suspected by the government of their country, and the acknowledgment that *since they parted* Booth had communicated, among other things, a suggestion which leads to the remark in this letter, "I would prefer your first query, 'Go and see how it will be taken at Richmond,' and *ere long*

I shall be better prepared *to again be with you.*" This is a declaration that affects Arnold, Booth, and O'Laughlin alike, if the court are satisfied, and it is difficult to see how they can have doubt on the subject, that the matter to be referred to Richmond is the matter of the assassination of the President and others, to effect which these parties had previously agreed and conspired together. It is a matter in testimony, by the declaration of John H. Surratt, who is as clearly proved to have been in this conspiracy and murder as Booth himself, that about the very date of this letter, the 27th of March, upon the suggestion of Booth, and with his knowledge and consent, he went to Richmond, not only to see "how it would be taken there," but to get funds with which to carry out the enterprise, as Booth had already declared to Chester in one of his last interviews, when he said that he or "some one of the party" would be constrained to go to Richmond for funds to carry out the conspiracy. Surratt returned from Richmond, bringing with him some part of the money for which he went, and was then going to Canada, and, as the testimony discloses, bringing with him the despatches from Jefferson Davis to his chief agents in Canada, which, as Thompson declared to Conover, made the proposed assassination "all right." Surratt, after seeing the parties here, left immediately for Canada and delivered his despatches to Jacob Thompson, the agent of Jefferson Davis. This was done by Surratt upon the suggestion, or in exact accordance with the suggestion, of Arnold, made on the 27th of March in his letter to Booth just read, and yet you are gravely told that four weeks before the 27th of March Arnold had abandoned the conspiracy.

Surratt reached Canada with these despatches, as we have seen, about the 6th or 7th of April last, when the witness Conover saw them delivered to Jacob Thompson and heard their contents stated by Thompson, and the declaration from him that these despatches made it "all right." That Surratt was at that time in Canada is not only established by the testimony of Conover, but it is also in evidence that he told Weichmann on the 3d of April that he was going to Canada, and on that day left for Canada, and afterwards, two letters addressed by Surratt over the *fictitious* signature of John Harrison, to his mother and to Miss Ward, dated at Montreal, were received by them on the 14th of April, as testified by Weichmann and by Miss Ward, a witness called for the defence. Thus it appears that the condition named by Arnold in his letter had been complied with. Booth had "gone to Richmond," in the person of Surratt, "to see how it would be taken." The rebel authorities at Richmond had approved it, the agent had returned, and Arnold was, in his own words, thereby the better prepared to rejoin Booth in the prosecution of this conspiracy.

To this end Arnold went to Fortress Monroe. As his letter expressly declares, Booth said when they parted, "we would not meet in a month or so, and *therefore* I made application for employment—an answer to which I shall receive during the week." He did receive the answer that week from Fortress Monroe, and went there to await the "more propitious time," bearing with him the weapon of death which Booth had provided and ready to obey his call, as the act had been approved at Richmond and been made " all right." Acting upon the same fact that the conspiracy had been approved in Richmond and the *funds* provided, O'Laughlin came to Washington to identify General Grant, the person who was to become the victim of his violence in the final consummation of this crime—General Grant, whom, as is averred in the specification, it had become the part of O'Laughlin by his agreement in this conspiracy to kill and murder. On the evening preceding the assassination—the 13th of April—by the testimony of three reputable witnesses, against whose truthfulness not one word is uttered here or elsewhere, O'Laughlin went into the house of the Secretary of War, where General Grant then was, and placed himself in position in the hall where he could see him, having declared before he reached that point to one of these witnesses that he wished to see General Grant. The house was brilliantly illuminated at the time; two at least of the witnesses conversed with the accused and the other stood very near to him, took special notice of his conduct, called attention to it, and suggested that he be put out of the house, and he was accordingly put out by one of the witnesses. These witnesses are confident, and have no doubt, and so swear upon their oaths, that Michael O'Laughlin is the man who was present on that occasion. There is no denial on the part of the accused that he was in Washington during the day and during the night of April 13, and also during the day and during the night of the 14th; and yet, to get rid of this testimony, recourse is had to that common device—an *alibi*; a device never, I may say, more frequently resorted to than in this trial. But what an *alibi!* Nobody is called to prove it, save some men who, by their own testimony, were engaged in a drunken debauch through the evening. A reasonable man who reads their evidence can hardly be expected to allow it to outweigh the united testimony of three unimpeached and unimpeachable witnesses who were clear in their statements, who entertain no doubt of the truth of what they say, whose opportunities to know were full and complete, and who were constrained to take special notice of the prisoner by reason of his extraordinary conduct.

These witnesses describe accurately the appearance, stature, and complexion of the accused, but because they describe his clothing as dark or black, it is urged that as part of his clothing, although dark, was not black, the witnesses are mistaken. O'Laughlin and his drunken companions (one of whom swears that he drank ten times that evening) were strolling in the streets and in the direction of the house of the Secretary of War, up the Avenue; but you are asked to believe that these witnesses could not be mistaken in saying they were not off the Avenue above 7th street, or on K street. I venture to say that no man who reads their testimony can determine satisfactorily all the places that were visited by O'Laughlin and his drunken associates that evening from 7 to 11 o'clock p. m. All this time, from 7 to 11 o'clock p. m., must be accounted for satisfactorily before the *alibi* can be established. Laughlan does not account for all the time, for he left O'Laughlin after 7 o'clock, and rejoined him, as he says, "I suppose about 8 o'clock." Grillet did not meet him until *half-past ten*, and then only casually saw him in passing the hotel. May not Grillet have been mistaken as to the fact, although he did meet O'Laughlin after 11 o'clock the same evening, as he swears?

Purdy swears to seeing him in the bar with Grillet about half-past 10, but, as we have seen by Grillet's testimony, it must have been after 11 o'clock. Murphy contradicts, *as to time*, both Grillet and Purdy, for he says it was half-past 11 or 12 o'clock when he and O'Laughlin returned to Rullman's from Platz's, and Early swears the accused went from Rullman's to 2d street to a dance about a quarter-past 11 o'clock, when O'Laughlin took the lead in the dance and stayed about one hour. I follow these witnesses no further. They contradict each other, and do not account for O'Laughlin all the time from 7 to 11 o'clock. I repeat that no man can read their testimony without finding contradictions most material *as to time*, and coming to the conviction that they utterly fail to account for O'Laughlin's whereabouts on that evening. To establish an *alibi* the witnesses *must know the fact* and *testify* to it. Laughlan, Grillet, Purdy, Murphy, and Early utterly fail to prove it, and only succeed in showing that they did not know where O'Laughlin was all this time, and that some of them were grossly mistaken in what they testified, both as to *time and place*. The testimony of James B. Henderson is equally unsatisfactory. He is contradicted by other testimony of the accused as *to place*. He says O'Laughlin went up the Avenue above 7th street, but that he did not go to 9th street. The other witnesses swear he went to 9th street. He swears he went to Canterbury about 9 o'clock, after going back from 7th street to Rullman's. Laughlan swears that O'Laughlin was with him at the corner of the Avenue and 9th street at 9 o'clock, and went from there to Canterbury, while Early swears that O'Laughlin went up as far as 11th street and returned with him and took supper at Welcker's about 8 o'clock. If these witnesses prove an *alibi*, it is really against each other. It is folly to pretend that they prove facts which make it impossible that O'Laughlin could have been at the house of Secretary Stanton, as three witnesses swear he was, on the evening of the 13th of April, looking for General Grant.

Has it not, by the testimony thus reviewed, been established *prima facie* that in the months of February, March, and April, O'Laughlin had combined, confederated, and agreed with John Wilkes Booth and Samuel Arnold to kill and murder Abraham Lincoln, William H. Seward, Andrew Johnson, and Ulysses S. Grant? Is it not established, beyond a shadow of doubt, that Booth had so conspired with the rebel agents in Canada as early as October last; that he was in search of agents to do the work *on pay*, in the interests of the rebellion, and that in this speculation Arnold and O'Laughlin had joined as early as February ; that then, and after, with Booth and Surratt, they were in the "oil business," which was the business of assassination by contract as a speculation ? If this conspiracy on the part of O'Laughlin with Arnold is established even *prima facie*, the declarations and acts of Arnold and Booth, the other conspirators, in furtherance of the common design, is evidence against O'Laughlin as well as against Arnold himself or the other parties. The rule of law is, that the act or declaration of one conspirator, done in pursuance or furtherance of the common design, is the act or declaration of all the conspirators. (1 Wharton, 706.)

The letter, therefore, of his co-conspirator, Arnold, is evidence against O'Laughlin, because it is an act in the prosecution of the common conspiracy, suggesting what should be done in order to make it effective, and which suggestion, as has been stated, was followed out. The defence has attempted to avoid the force of this letter by reciting the statement of Arnold, made to Horner at the time he was arrested, in which he declared, among other things, that the purpose was to abduct President Lincoln and take him south; that it was to be done at the theatre by throwing the President out of the box upon the floor of the stage, when the accused was to catch him. The very announcement of this testimony excited derision that such a tragedy meant only to take the President and carry him gently away! This pigmy to catch the giant as the assassins hurled him to the floor from an elevation of twelve feet! The court has viewed the theatre, and must be satisfied that Booth, in leaping from the President's box, broke his limb. The court cannot fail to conclude that this statement of Arnold was but another silly device, like that of "the oil business," which, for the time being, he employed to hide from the knowledge of his captor the fact that the purpose was to murder the President. No man can, for a moment, believe that any one of these conspirators hoped or desired, by such a proceeding as that stated by this prisoner, to take the President alive in the presence of thousands assembled in the theatre after he had been thus thrown upon the floor of the stage, much less to carry him through the city, through the lines of your army, and deliver him into the hands of the rebels. No such purpose was expressed or hinted by the conspirators in Canada, who commissioned Booth to let these assassinations on contract. I shall waste not a moment more in combatting such an absurdity.

Arnold does confess that he was a conspirator with Booth in this purposed murder; that Booth had a letter of introduction to Dr. Mudd; that Booth, O'Laughlin, Atzerodt, Surratt, a man with an alias, "Mosby," and another whom he does not know, and himself, were parties to this conspiracy, and that Booth had furnished them all with arms. He concludes this remarkable statement to Horner with the declaration that at that time, to wit, the first week of March, or four weeks before he went to Fortress Monroe, he left the conspiracy, and that Booth told him to sell his arms if he chose. This is sufficiently answered by the fact that, four weeks *afterwards*, he wrote his letter to Booth, which was found in Booth's possession after the assassination, suggesting to him what to do in order to make the conspiracy a success, and by the further fact that at the very moment he uttered these declarations, part of his arms were found upon his person, and the rest not disposed of, but at his father's house.

A party to a treasonable and murderous conspiracy against the government of his country cannot be held to have abandoned it because he makes such a declaration as this, when he is in the hands of the officer of the law, arrested for his crime, and especially when his declaration is in conflict with and expressly contradicted by his written acts, and unsupported by any conduct of his which becomes a citizen and a man.

If he abandoned the conspiracy, why did he not make known the fact to Abraham Lincoln and his constitutional advisers that these men, armed with the weapons of assassination, were daily lying in wait for their lives? To pretend that a man who thus conducts himself for weeks after the pretended abandonment, volunteering advice for the successful prosecution of the conspiracy, the evidence of which is in writing, and about which there can be no mistake, has, in fact, abandoned it, is to insult the common understanding of men. O'Laughlin having conspired with Arnold to do this murder, is, therefore, as much concluded by the letter of Arnold of the 27th of March as is Arnold himself. The further testimony touching O'Laughlin, that of Streett, establishes the fact that about the 1st of April he saw him in confidential conversation with J. Wilkes Booth, in this city, on the Avenue. Another man, whom the witness does not know, was in conversation. O'Laughlin called Streett to one side, and told him Booth was busily engaged with his friend—was *talking privately* to his friend. This remark of O'Laughlin is attempted to be accounted for, but the attempt failed; his counsel taking the pains to ask what induced O'Laughlin to make the remark, received the fit reply: "I did not see the interior of Mr. O'Laughlin's mind; I cannot tell." It is the province of this court to infer why that remark was made, and what it signified.

That John H. Surratt, George A. Atzerodt, Mary E. Surratt, David E. Herold, and Louis Payne, entered into this conspiracy with Booth, is so very clear upon the testimony, that little time need be occupied in bringing again before the court the evidence which establishes it. By the testimony of Weichmann we find Atzerodt in February at the house of the prisoner, Mrs. Surratt. He inquired for her or for John when he came and remained over night. After this and before the assassination he visited there frequently, and at that house bore the name of "Port Tobacco," the name by which he was known in Canada among the conspirators there. The same witness testifies that he met him on the street, when he said he was going to visit Payne at the Herndon House, and also accompanied him, along with Herold and John H. Surratt, to the theatre in March to hear Booth play in the Apostate. At the Pennsylvania House, one or two weeks previous to the assassination, Atzerodt made the statement to Lieutenant Keim, when asking for his knife which he had left in his room, a knife corresponding in size with the one exhibited in court, "I want that; if one fails I want the other," wearing at the same time his revolver at his belt. He also stated to Greenawalt, of the Pennsylvania House, in March, that he was nearly broke, but had friends enough to give him as much money as *would see him through*, adding, "I am going away some of these days, but will return with as much gold as will keep me all my lifetime." Mr. Greenawalt also says that Booth had frequent interviews with Atzerodt, sometimes in the room, and at other times Booth would walk in and immediately go out, Atzerodt following.

John M. Lloyd testifies that some six weeks before the assassination, Herold, Atzerodt, and John H. Surratt came to his house at Surrattsville, bringing with them two Spencer carbines with ammunition, also a rope and wrench. Surratt asked the witness to take care of them, and to conceal the carbines. Surratt took him into a room in the house, it being his mother's house, and showed the witness where to put the carbines, between the joists on the second floor. The carbines were put there according to his directions, and concealed. Marcus P. Norton saw Atzerodt in conversation with Booth at the National Hotel about the 2d or 3d of March; the conversation was confidential, and the witness accidentally heard them talking in regard to President Johnson, and say that "the class of witnesses would be of that character that there could be little proven by them." This conversation may throw some light on the fact that Atzerodt was found in possession of Booth's bank book!

Colonel Nevens testifies that on the 12th of April last he saw Atzerodt at the Kirkwood House; that Atzerodt there asked him, a stranger, if he knew where Vice President Johnson was, and where Mr. Johnson's *room was*. Colonel Nevens showed him where the room of the Vice President was, and told him that the Vice President was then at dinner. Atzerodt then looked into the dining-room, where Vice President Johnson was dining alone. Robert R. Jones, the clerk at the Kirkwood House, states that on the 14th, the day of the murder, two days after this, Atzerodt registered his name at the hotel, G. A. Atzerodt, and took No. 126, retaining the room that day, and carrying away the key. In this room, after the assassination, were found the knife and revolver with which he intended to murder the Vice President.

The testimony of all these witnesses leaves no doubt that the prisoner George A. Atzerodt entered into this conspiracy with Booth ; that he expected to receive a large compensation for the service that he would render in its execution ; that he had undertaken the assassination of the Vice President for a price ; that he, with Surratt and Herold, rendered the important service of depositing the arms and ammunition to be used by Booth and his confederates as a protection in their flight after the conspiracy had been executed ; and that he was careful to have his intended victim pointed out to him, and the room he occupied in the hotel, so that when he came to perform his horrid work he would know precisely where to go and whom to strike.

I take no further notice now of the preparation which this prisoner made for the successful execution of this part of the traitorous and murderous design. The question is, did he enter into this conspiracy ? His language overheard by Mr. Norton excludes every other conclusion. Vice President Johnson's name was mentioned in that secret conversation with Booth, and the very suggestive expression was made between them that "little could be proved by the witnesses." His confession in his defence is conclusive of his guilt.

That Payne was in this conspiracy is confessed in the defence made by his counsel, and is also evident from the facts proved, that when the conspiracy was being organized in Canada by Thompson, Sanders, Tucker, Cleary, and Clay, this man Payne stood at the door of Thompson ; was recommended and indorsed by Clay with the words, " We trust him ;" that after coming hither he first reported himself at the house of Mrs. Mary E. Surratt, inquired for her and for John H. Surratt, remained there for four days, having conversation with both of them ; having provided himself with means of disguise, was also supplied with pistols and a knife, such as he afterwards used, and spurs, preparatory to his flight ; was seen with John H. Surratt, practicing with knives such as those employed in this deed of assassination, and now before the court ; was afterwards provided with lodging at the Herndon House, at the instance of Surratt ; was visited there by Atzerodt, and attended Booth and Surratt to Ford's theatre, occupying with those parties the box, as I believe and which we may readily infer, in which the President was afterwards murdered.

If further testimony be wanting that he had entered into the conspiracy, it may be found in the fact sworn to by Weichmann, whose testimony no candid man will discredit, that about the 20th of March Mrs. Surratt, in great excitement, and weeping, said that her son

John had gone away not to return, when about three hours subsequently, in the afternoon of the same day, John H. Surratt reappeared, came rushing in a state of frenzy into the room, in his mother's house, armed, declaring he would shoot whoever came into the room, and proclaiming that his prospects were blasted and his hopes gone; that soon Payne came into the same room, also armed and under great excitement, and was immediately followed by Booth, with his riding-whip in his hand, who walked rapidly across the floor from side to side, so much excited that for some time he did not notice the presence of the witness. Observing Weichmann the parties then withdrew, upon a suggestion from Booth, to an upper room, and there had a private interview. From all that transpired on that occasion, it is apparent that when these parties left the house that day, it was with the full purpose of completing some act essential to the final execution of the work of assassination, in conformity with their previous confederation and agreement. They returned foiled—from what cause is unknown—dejected, angry, and covered with confusion.

It is almost imposing upon the patience of the court to consume time in demonstrating the fact, which none conversant with the testimony of this case can for a moment doubt, that John H. Surratt and Mary E. Surratt were as surely in the conspiracy to murder the President as was John Wilkes Booth himself. You have the frequent interviews between John H. Surratt and Booth, his intimate relations with Payne, his visits from Atzerodt and Herold, his deposit of the arms to cover their flight after the conspiracy should have been executed; his own declared visit to Richmond to do what Booth himself said to Chester must be done, to wit, that he or some of the party must go to Richmond in order to get funds to carry out the conspiracy; that he brought back with him gold, the price of blood, confessing himself that he was there; that he immediately went to Canada, delivered despatches in cipher to Jacob Thompson from Jefferson Davis, which were interpreted and read by Thompson in the presence of the witness Conover, and in which the conspiracy was approved, and, in the language of Thompson, the proposed assassination was "made all right."

One other fact, if any other fact be needed, and I have done with the evidence which proves that John H. Surratt entered into this combination; that is, that it appears by the testimony of the witness, the cashier of the Ontario Bank, Montreal, that Jacob Thompson, about the day that these despatches were delivered, and while Surratt was then present in Canada, drew from that bank of the rebel funds there on deposit the sum of one hundred and eighty thousand dollars. This being done, Surratt finding it safer, doubtless, to go to Canada for the great bulk of funds which were to be distributed amongst these hired assassins than to attempt to carry it through our lines direct from Richmond, immediately returned to Washington and was present in this city, as is proven by the testimony of Mr. Reid, *on the afternoon of the* 14*th of April*, the day of the assassination, booted and spurred, ready for the flight whenever the fatal blow should have been struck. If he was not a conspirator and a party to this great crime, how comes it that from that hour to this no man has seen him in the capital, nor has he been reported anywhere outside of Canada, having arrived at Montreal, as the testimony shows, on the 18th of April, four days after the murder? Nothing but his conscious coward guilt could possibly induce him to absent himself from his mother, as he does, upon her trial. Being one of these conspirators, as charged, every act of his in the prosecution of this crime is evidence against the other parties to the conspiracy.

That Mary E. Surratt is as guilty as her son of having thus conspired, combined, and confederated to do this murder, in aid of this rebellion, is clear. First, her house was the headquarters of Booth, John H. Surratt, Atzerodt, Payne, and Herold. She is inquired for by Atzerodt; she is inquired for by Payne; and she is visited by Booth, and holds private conversations with him. His picture, together with that of the chief conspirator, Jefferson Davis, is found in her house. She sends to Booth for a carriage to take her, on the 11th of April, to Surrattsville for the purpose of perfecting the arrangement deemed necessary to the successful execution of the conspiracy, and especially to facilitate and protect the conspirators in their escape from justice. On that occasion Booth, having disposed of his carriage, gives to the agent she employed ten dollars with which to hire a conveyance for that purpose. And yet the pretence is made that Mrs. Surratt went on the 11th to Surrattsville exclusively upon her own private and lawful business. Can any one tell, if that be so, how it comes that she should apply *to Booth* for a conveyance, and how it comes that he, of his own accord, having no conveyance to furnish her, should send her ten dollars with which to procure it? There is not the slightest indication that Booth was under any obligation to her, or that she had any claim upon him, either for a conveyance or for the means with which to procure one, except that he was bound to contribute, being the agent of the conspirators in Canada and Richmond, whatever money might be necessary to the consummation of this infernal plot. On that day, the 11th of April, John H. Surratt had not returned from Canada with the funds furnished by Thompson!

Upon that journey of the 11th the accused, Mary E. Surratt, met the witness John M. Lloyd at Uniontown. She called him; he got out of his carriage and came to her, and she whispered to him in so low a tone that her attendant could not hear her words, though Lloyd, to whom they were spoken, did distinctly hear them, and testifies that she told him he should have those "shooting-irons" ready, meaning the carbines which her son and Herold and Atzerodt had deposited with him, and added the reason, "for they would soon be called for." On the day of the assassination she again sent for Booth, had an interview with him in her own house, and immediately went again to Surrattsville, and then, at about six o'clock in the afternoon, she delivered to Lloyd a field-glass and told him "to have two bottles of whiskey and the carbines ready, as they would be called for that night." Having thus perfected the arrangement she returned to Washington to her own house, at about half-past eight o'clock in the evening, to await the final result. How could this woman anticipate on Friday afternoon, at six o'clock, that these arms would be called for and would be needed that night unless she was in the conspiracy and knew the blow was to be struck, and the flight of the assassins attempted and by that route? Was not the private conversation which Booth held with her in her parlor on the afternoon of the 14th of April, just before she left on this business, in relation to the orders she should give to have the arms ready?

An endeavor is made to impeach Lloyd. But the court will observe that no witness has been called who contradicts Lloyd's statement in any material matter; neither has his general character for truth been assailed. How, then, is he impeached? Is it claimed that his testimony shows that he was a party to the conspiracy? Then it is conceded by those who set up any such pretence that there was a conspiracy. A conspiracy between whom? There can be no conspiracy without the co-operation or agreement of two or more persons. Who were the other parties to it? Was it Mary E. Surratt? Was it John H. Surratt, George A. Atzerodt, David E. Herold? Those are the only persons, so far as his own testimony or the testimony of any other witness discloses, with whom he had any communication whatever on any subject immediately or remotely touching this conspiracy before the assassination. His receipt and concealment of the arms are, unexplained, evidence that he was in the conspiracy.

The explanation is that he was dependent upon Mary E. Surratt; was her tenant; and his declaration, given in evidence by the accused herself, is that "she had ruined him, and brought this trouble upon him." But because he was weak enough, or wicked enough, to become the guilty depositary of these arms, and to deliver them on the order of Mary E. Surratt to the assassins, it does not follow that he is not to be believed on oath. It is said that he concealed the facts that the arms had been left and called for. He so testifies himself, but he gives the reason that he did it only from apprehension of danger to his life. If he were in the conspiracy, his general credit being unchallenged, his testimony being uncontradicted in any material matter, he is to be believed, and cannot be disbelieved if his testimony is substantially corroborated by other reliable witnesses. Is he not corroborated touching the deposit of arms by the fact that the arms are produced in court—one of which was found upon the person of Booth at the time he was overtaken and slain, and which is identified as the same which had been left with Lloyd by Herold, Surratt, and Atzerodt? Is he not corroborated in the fact of the first interview with Mrs. Surratt by the joint testimony of Mrs. Offut and Lewis J. Weichmann, each of whom testified, (and they are contradicted by no one,) that on Tuesday, the 11th day of April, at Uniontown, Mrs. Surratt called Mr. Lloyd to come to her, which he did, and she held a *secret* conversation with him? Is he not corroborated as to the last conversation on the 14th of April by the testimony of Mrs. Offut, who swears that upon the evening of the 14th of April she saw the prisoner, Mary E. Surratt, at Lloyd's house, approach and hold conversation with him? Is he not corroborated in the fact, to which he swears, that Mrs. Surratt delivered to him at that time the field-glass wrapped in paper, by the sworn statement of Weichmann that Mrs. Surratt took with her on that occasion two packages, both of which were wrapped in paper, and one of which he describes as a small package about six inches in diameter? The attempt was made by calling Mrs. Offut to prove that no such package was delivered, but it failed; she merely states that Mrs. Surratt delivered a package wrapped in paper to her after her arrival there, and before Lloyd came in, which was laid down in the room. But whether it was *the* package about which Lloyd testifies, or the other package of the *two* about which Weichmann testifies, as having been carried there that day by Mrs. Surratt, does not appear. Neither does this witness pretend to say that Mrs. Surratt, after she had delivered it to her, and the witness had laid it down in the room, did not again take it up, if it were the same, and put it in the hands of Lloyd. She only knows that she did not see that done; but she did see Lloyd with a package like the one she received in the room before Mrs. Surratt left. How it came into his possession she is not able to state; nor what the package was that Mrs. Surratt first handed her; nor which of the packages it was she afterwards saw in the hands of Lloyd.

But there is one other fact in this case that puts forever at rest the question of the guilty participation of the prisoner Mrs. Surratt in this conspiracy and murder; and that is that Payne, who had lodged four days in her house—who during all that time had sat at her table, and who had often conversed with her—when the guilt of his great crime was upon him, and he knew not where else he could so safely go to find a co-conspirator, and he could trust none that was not like himself, guilty, with even the knowledge of his presence—under cover of darkness, after wandering for three days and nights, skulking before the pursuing officers of justice, at the hour of midnight, found his way to the door of Mrs. Surratt, rang the bell, was admitted, and upon being asked, "Whom do you want to see," replied, "Mrs. Surratt." He was then asked by the officer Morgan, what he came at that time of night for? to which he replied, "to dig a gutter in the morning; Mrs. Surratt had sent for him." Afterwards he said "Mrs. Surratt knew he was a poor man and *came to him.*" Being asked where he last worked? he replied, "sometimes on 'I' street;" and where he boarded? he replied, "he had no boarding-house, and was a poor man who got his living with the pick," which he bore upon his shoulder, having stolen it from the intrenchments of the capital. Upon being pressed again why he came there at that time of night to go to work, he answered that he simply called to see what time he should go to work in the morning. Upon being told by the officer who fortunately had preceded him to this house that he would have to go to the provost marshal's office, he moved and did not answer, whereupon Mrs. Surratt was asked to step into the hall and state whether she knew this man. Raising her right hand she exclaimed, "Before God, sir, I have not seen that man before; I have not hired him; I do not know anything about him." The hall was brilliantly lighted.

If not one word had been said, the mere act of Payne in flying to her house for shelter would have borne witness against her, strong as proofs from Holy Writ. But when she denies, after hearing his declarations, that she had sent for him, or that she had gone to him and hired him, and calls her God to witness that she had never seen him, and knew nothing of him, when, in point of fact, she had seen him for four successive days in her own house, in the same clothing which he then wore, who can resist for a moment the conclusion that these parties were alike guilty?

The testimony of Spangler's complicity is conclusive and brief. It was impossible to hope for escape after assassinating the President, and such others as might attend him in Ford's theatre, without arrangements being first made to aid the flight of the assassin and to some extent prevent immediate pursuit.

A stable was to be provided close to Ford's theatre, in which the horses could be concealed and kept ready for the assassin's use whenever the murderous blow was struck. Accordingly, Booth secretly, through Maddox, hired a stable in rear of the theatre and connecting with it by an alley, as early as the 1st of January last; showing that at that time he had concluded, notwithstanding all that has been said to the contrary, to murder the President in Ford's theatre and provide the means for immediate and successful flight. Conscious of his guilt, he paid the rent for this stable through Maddox, month by month, giving him the money. He employed Spangler, doubtless for the reason that he could trust him with the secret, as a carpenter to fit up this shed, so that it would furnish room for two horses, and provided the door with lock and key. Spangler did this work for him. Then, it was necessary that a carpenter having access to the theatre should be employed by the assassin to provide a bar for the outer door of the passage leading to the President's box, so that when he entered upon his work of assassination he would be secure from interruption from the rear. By the evidence, it is shown that Spangler was in the box in which the President was murdered on the afternoon of the 14th of April, and when there damned the President and General Grant, and said the President ought to be cursed, he had got so many good men killed; showing not only his hostility to the President, but the cause of it—that he had been faithful to his oath and had resisted that great rebellion in the interest of which his life was about to be sacrificed by this man and his co-conspirators. In performing the work which had doubtless been intrusted to him by Booth, a mortise was cut in the wall. A wooden bar was prepared, one end of which could be readily inserted in the mortise and the other pressed against the edge of the door on the inside so as to prevent its being opened. Spangler had the skill and the opportunity to do that work and all the additional work which was done.

It is in evidence that the screws in "the keepers" to the locks on each of the inner doors of the box occupied by the President were drawn. The attempt has been made, on behalf of the prisoner, to show that this was done some time before, accidentally, and with no bad design, and had not been repaired by reason of inadvertence; but that attempt has utterly failed, because the testimony adduced for that purpose relates exclusively to but one of the two inner doors, while the fact is, that the screws were drawn in *both*, and the additional precaution taken to cut a small hole through one of these doors through which the party approaching and while in the private passage would be enabled to look into the box and examine the exact posture of the President before entering. It was also deemed essential, in the execution of this plot, that some one should watch at the outer door, in the rear of the theatre, by which alone the assassin could hope for escape. It was for this work Booth sought to employ Chester in January, offering $3,000 down of the money of his employers, and the assurance that he should never want. What Chester refused to do Spangler undertook and promised to do. When Booth brought his horse to the rear door of the theatre, on the evening of the murder, he called for Spangler, who went to him, when Booth was heard to say to him, "Ned, you'll help me all you can, won't you." To which Spangler replied, "Oh, yes."

When Booth made his escape, it is testified by Colonel Stewart, who pursued him across the stage and out through the same door, that as he approached it some one slammed it shut. Ritterspaugh, who was standing behind the scenes when Booth fired the pistol and fled, saw Booth run down the passage toward the back door, and pursued him; but Booth drew his knife upon him and passed out, slamming the door after him. Ritterspaugh opened it and went through, leaving *it open* behind him, leaving Spangler inside, and in a position from which he readily could have reached the door. Ritterspaugh also states that very quickly after he had passed through this door he was followed by a large man, the first who followed him, and who was, doubtless, Colonel Stewart. Stewart is very positive that he saw this door slammed; that he himself was constrained to open it, and had some difficulty in opening it. He also testifies that as he approached the door a man stood near enough to have thrown it to with his hand, and this man, the witness believes, was the prisoner Spangler. Ritterspaugh has sworn that he left the door open behind him when he went out, and that he was first followed by the large man, Colonel Stewart. Who slammed that door behind Ritterspaugh? It was not Ritterspaugh; it could not have been Booth, for Ritterspaugh swears that Booth was mounting his horse at the time; and Stewart swears that Booth was upon his horse when he came out. That it was Spangler who slammed the door after Ritterspaugh may not only be inferred from Stewart's testimony, but it is made very clear by his own conduct afterwards upon the return of Ritterspaugh to the stage. The door being then open, and Ritterspaugh being asked which way Booth went, had answered. Ritterspaugh says: "Then I came back on the stage, where I had left Edward Spangler; he hit me on the face with his hand and said, 'Don't say which way he went.' I asked him what he meant by slapping me in the mouth? He said, 'For God's sake, shut up.'"

The testimony of Withers is adroitly handled to throw doubt upon these facts. It cannot avail, for Withers says he was knocked in the scene by Booth, and when he "come to" he got a side view of him. A man knocked down and senseless, on "coming to" might mistake anybody by a side view for Booth.

An attempt has been made by the defence to discredit this testimony of Ritterspaugh, by showing his contradictory statements to Gifford, Carlan, and Lamb, neither of whom do in fact contradict him, but substantially sustain him. None but a guilty man would have met the witness with a blow for stating which way the assassin had gone. A like confession of guilt was made by Spangler when the witness Miles, the same evening, and directly after the assassination, came to the back door, where Spangler was standing with others, and asked Spangler who it was that held the horse, to which Spangler replied: "Hush; don't say anything about it." He confessed his guilt again when he denied to Mary Anderson the fact, proved here beyond all question, that Booth had called him when he came to that door with his horse, using the emphatic words, "No, he did not; he did not call me." The rope comes to bear witness against him, as did the rope which Atzerodt and Herold and John H. Surratt had carried to Surrattsville and deposited there with the carbines.

It is only surprising that the ingenious counsel did not attempt to explain the deposit of the rope at Surrattsville by the same method that he adopted in explanation of the deposit of this rope, some sixty feet long, found in the carpet-sack of Spangler, unaccounted for save by some evidence which tends to show that he may have carried it away from the theatre.

It is not needful to take time in the recapitulation of the evidence, which shows conclusively that David E. Herold was one of these conspirators. His continued association with Booth, with Atzerodt, his visits to Mrs. Surratt's, his attendance at the theatre with Payne, Surratt, and Atzerodt, his connexion with Atzerodt on the evening of the murder, riding with him on the street in the direction of and near to the theatre at the hour appointed for the work of assassination, and his final flight and arrest, show that he, in common with all the other parties on trial, and all the parties named upon your record not upon trial, had combined and confederated to kill and murder in the interests of the rebellion, as charged and specified against them.

That this conspiracy was entered into by all these parties, both present and absent, is thus proved by the acts, meetings, declarations, and correspondence of all the parties, beyond any doubt whatever. True it is circumstantial evidence, but the court will remember the rule before recited, that circumstances cannot lie; that they are held sufficient in every court where justice is judicially administered to establish the fact of a conspiracy. I shall take no further notice of the remark made by the learned counsel who opened for the defence, and which has been followed by several of his associates, that, under the Constitution, it requires two witnesses to prove the overt act of high treason, than to say, this is not a charge of high treason, but of a treasonable conspiracy, in aid of a rebellion, with intent to kill and murder the executive officer of the United States, and commander of its armies, and of the murder of the President in pursuance of that conspiracy, and with the intent laid, &c. Neither by the Constitution, nor by the rules of the common law, is any fact connected with this allegation required to be established by the testimony of more than one witness. I might say, however, that every substantive averment against each of the parties named upon this record has been established by the testimony of more than one witness.

That the several accused did enter into this conspiracy with John Wilkes Booth and John H. Surratt to murder the officers of this government named upon the record, in pursuance of the wishes of their employers and instigators in Richmond and Canada, and with intent thereby to aid the existing rebellion and subvert the Constitution and laws of the United States, as alleged, is no longer an open question.

The intent as laid was expressly declared by Sanders in the meeting of the conspirators at Montreal in February last, by Booth in

Virginia and New York, and by Thompson to Conover and Montgomery; but if there were no testimony directly upon this point, the law would presume the intent, for the reason that such was the natural and necessary tendency and manifest design of the act itself.

The learned gentleman (Mr. Johnson) says the government has survived the assassination of the President, and thereby would have you infer that this conspiracy was not entered into and attempted to be executed with the intent laid. With as much show of reason it might be said that because the government of the United States has survived this unmatched rebellion, it therefore results that the rebel conspirators waged war upon the government with no purpose or intent thereby to subvert it. By the law we have seen that without any direct evidence of previous combination and agreement between these parties, the conspiracy might be established by evidence of the acts of the prisoners, or of any others with whom they co-operated, concurring in the execution of the common design. (Roscoe, 416.)

Was there co-operation between the several accused in the execution of this conspiracy? That there was is as clearly established by the testimony as is the fact that Abraham Lincoln was killed and murdered by John Wilkes Booth. The evidence shows that all of the accused, save Mudd and Arnold, were in Washington on the 14th of April, the day of the assassination, together with John Wilkes Booth and John H. Surratt; that on that day Booth had a secret interview with the prisoner Mary E. Surratt; that immediately thereafter she went to Surrattsville to perform her part of the preparation necessary to the successful execution of the conspiracy, and did make that preparation; that John H. Surratt had arrived here from Canada, notifying the parties that the price to be paid for this great crime had been provided for, at least in part, by the deposit receipts of April 6th for $180,000, procured by Thompson of the Ontario Bank, Montreal, Canada; that he was also prepared to keep watch, or strike a blow, and ready for the contemplated flight; that Atzerodt, on the afternoon of that day, was seeking to obtain a horse, the better to secure his own safety by flight, after he should have performed the task which he had voluntarily undertaken by contract in the conspiracy—the murder of Andrew Johnson, then Vice President of the United States; that he did procure a horse for that purpose at Naylor's, and was seen about nine o'clock in the evening to ride to the Kirkwood House, where the Vice President then was, dismount, and enter. At a previous hour Booth was in the Kirkwood

House, and left his card, now in evidence, doubtless intended to be sent to the room of the Vice President, and which was in these words: "Don't wish to disturb you. Are you at home? J. Wilkes Booth." Atzerodt, when he made application at Brooks's in the afternoon for the horse, said to Weichmann, who was there, he was going to ride in the country, and that "he was going to get a horse and send for Payne." He did get a horse for Payne, as well as for himself; for it is proven that on the 12th he was seen in Washington riding the horse which had been procured by Booth, in company with Mudd, last November, from Gardner. A similar horse was tied before the door of Mr. Seward on the night of the murder, was captured after the flight of Payne, who was seen to ride away, and which horse is now identified as the Gardner horse. Booth also procured a horse on the same day, took it to his stable in the rear of the theatre, where he had an interview with Spangler, and where he concealed it. Herold, too, obtained a horse in the afternoon, and was seen between nine and ten o'clock riding with Atzerodt down the Avenue from the Treasury, then up Fourteenth and down F street, passing close by Ford's theatre.

O'Laughlin had come to Washington the day before, had sought out his victim (General Grant) at the house of the Secretary of War, that he might be able with certainty to identify him, and at the very hour when these preparations were going on was lying in wait at Rullman's, on the Avenue, keeping watch, and declaring, as he did, at about 10 o'clock p. m., when told that the fatal blow had been struck by Booth, "I don't believe Booth did it." During the day, and the night before, he had been visiting Booth, and doubtless encouraging him, and at that very hour was in position, at a convenient distance, to aid and protect him in his flight, as well as to execute his own part of the conspiracy by inflicting death upon General Grant, who happily was not at the theatre nor in the city, having left the city that day. Who doubts that, Booth having ascertained in the course of the day that General Grant would not be present at the theatre, O'Laughlin, who was to murder General Grant, instead of entering the box with Booth, was detailed to lie in wait, and watch and support him.

His declarations of his reasons for changing his lodgings here and in Baltimore, after the murder, so ably and so ingeniously presented in the argument of his learned counsel, (Mr. Cox,) avail nothing before the blasting fact that he did change his lodgings, and declared "he knew nothing of the affair whatever." O'Laughlin, who lurked here, conspiring daily with Booth and Arnold for six weeks to do this murder, declares "he knew nothing of the affair." O'Laughlin, who said he was "in the oil business," which Booth and Surratt, and Payne and Arnold, have all declared meant this conspiracy, says he "knew nothing of the affair." O'Laughlin, to whom Booth sent the despatches of the 13th and 27th of March—O'Laughlin, who is named in Arnold's letter as one of the conspirators, and who searched for General Grant on Thursday night, laid in wait for him on Friday, was defeated by that Providence "which shapes our ends," and laid in wait to aid Booth and Payne, declares "he knows nothing of the matter." Such a denial is as false and inexcusable as Peter's denial of our Lord.

Mrs. Surratt had arrived at home, from the completion of her part in the plot, about half-past eight o'clock in the evening. A few moments afterwards she was called to the parlor and there had a private interview with some one unseen, but whose retreating footsteps were heard by the witness Weichmann. This was doubtless the secret and last visit of John H. Surratt to his mother, who had instigated and encouraged him to strike this traitorous and murderous blow against his country.

While all these preparations were going on, Mudd was awaiting the execution of the plot, ready to faithfully perform his part in securing the safe escape of the murderers. Arnold was at his post at Fortress Monroe, awaiting the meeting referred to in his letter of March 27th, wherein he says they were not "to meet for a month or so," which month had more than expired on the day of the murder, for his letter and the testimony disclose that this month of suspension began to run from about the first week in March. He stood ready with the arms which Booth had furnished him to aid the escape of the murderers by *that route*, and secure their communication with their employers. He had given the assurance in that letter to Booth, that although the government "suspicioned them," and the undertaking was "becoming complicated," yet "a time more propitious would arrive" for the consummation of this conspiracy in which he "was one" with Booth, and when he would "be better prepared to again be with him."

Such were the preparations. The horses were in readiness for the flight; the ropes were procured, doubtless for the purpose of tying the horses at whatever point they might be constrained to delay and to secure their boats to their moorings in making their way across the Potomac. The five murderous camp knives, the two carbines, the eight revolvers, the Derringer, in court and identified, all were ready for the work of death. The part that each had played has already been in part stated in this argument, and needs no repetition.

Booth proceeded to the theatre about 9 o'clock in the evening, at the same time that Atzerodt and Payne and Herold were riding the streets, while Surratt, having parted with his mother at the brief interview in her parlor, from which his retreating steps were heard, was walking the Avenue, booted and spurred, and doubtless consulting with O'Laughlin. When Booth reached the rear of the theatre, he called Spangler to him, (whose denial of that fact, when charged with it, as proven by three witnesses, is very significant,) and received from Spangler his pledge to help him all he could, when with Booth he entered the theatre by the stage-door, doubtless to see that the way was clear from the box to the rear door of the theatre, and look upon their victim, whose exact position they could study from the stage. After this view, Booth passes to the street, in front of the theatre, where, on the pavement with other conspirators yet unknown, among them one described as a low-browed villain, he awaits the appointed moment. Booth himself, impatient, enters the vestibule of the theatre from the front, and asks the time. He is referred to the clock, and returns. Presently, as the hour of 10 o'clock approached, one of his guilty associates called the time: they wait; again, as the moments elapsed, this conspirator upon watch called the time; again, as the appointed hour draws nigh, he calls the time; and finally, when the fatal moment arrives, he repeats in a louder tone, "Ten minutes past 10 o'clock." Ten minutes past 10 o'clock! The hour has come when the red right hand of these murderous conspirators should strike, and the dreadful deed of assassination be done.

Booth, at the appointed moment, entered the theatre, ascended to the dress-circle, passed to the right, paused a moment, looking down, doubtless to see if Spangler was at his post, and approached the outer door of the close passage leading to the box occupied by the President, pressed it open, passed in, and closed the passage door behind him. Spangler's bar was in its place, and was readily adjusted by Booth in the mortise, and pressed against the inner side of the door, so that he was secure from interruption from without. He passes on to the next door, immediately behind the President, and there stopping, looks through the aperture in the door into the President's box, and deliberately observes the precise position of his victim, seated in the chair which had been prepared by the conspirators as the altar for the sacrifice, looking calmly and quietly down upon the glad and grateful people whom by his fidelity he had saved from the peril which had threatened the destruction of their government, and all they held dear this side of the grave, and whom he had come upon invitation to greet with his presence, with the words still lingering upon his lips which he had uttered with uncovered head and uplifted hand before God and his country, when on the 4th of last March he took again the oath to preserve, protect, and defend the Constitution, declaring that he entered upon the duties of his great office "with malice toward none—with charity for all." In a moment more, strengthened by the knowledge that his co-conspirators were all at their posts, seven at least of them present in the city, two of them, Mudd and Arnold, at their appointed places, watching for his coming, this hired assassin moves stealthily through the door, the fastenings of which had been removed to facilitate his entrance, fires upon his victim, and the martyr spirit of Abraham Lincoln ascends to God.

"Treason has done his worst; nor steel, nor poison,
Malice domestic, foreign levy, nothing
Can touch him further."

At the same hour, when these accused and their co-conspirators in Richmond and Canada, by the hand of John Wilkes Booth, inflicted this mortal wound which deprived the republic of its defender, and filled this land from ocean to ocean with a strange, great sorrow, Payne, a very demon in human form, with the words of falsehood upon his lips, that he was the bearer of a message from the physician of the venerable Secretary of State, sweeps by his servant, encounters his son, who protests that the assassin shall not disturb his father, prostrate on a bed of sickness, and receives for answer the assassin's blow from the revolver in his hand, repeated again and again, rushes into the room, is encountered by Major Seward, inflicts wound after wound upon him with his murderous knife, is encountered by Hansell and Robinson, each of whom he also wounds, springs upon the defenceless and feeble Secretary of State, stabs first on one side of his throat, then on the other, again in the face, and is only prevented from literally hacking out his life by the persistence and courage of the attendant Robinson. He turns to flee, and, his giant arm and murderous hand for a moment paralyzed by the consciousness of guilt, he drops his weapons of death, one in the house, the other at the door, where they were taken up, and are here now to bear witness against him. He attempts escape on the horse which Booth and Mudd had procured of Gardner—with what success has already been stated.

Atzerodt, near midnight, returns to the stable of Naylor the horse which he had procured for this work of murder, having been interrupted in the execution of the part assigned him at the Kirkwood House by the timely coming of citizens to the defence of the Vice President, and creeps into the Pennsylvania House at 2 o'clock in the morning with another of the conspirators, yet unknown. There he remained until about 5 o'clock, when he left, found his way to Georgetown, pawned one of his revolvers, now in court, and fled northward into Maryland.

He is traced to Montgomery county, to the house of Mr. Metz, on the Sunday succeeding the murder, where, as is proved by the testimony of three witnesses, he said that if the man that was to follow General Grant *had* followed him, it was likely that Grant was shot. To one of these witnesses (Mr. Layman) he said he did not think Grant had been killed; or if he had been killed, he was killed by a man who got on the cars at the same time that Grant did; thus disclosing most clearly that one of his co-conspirators was assigned the task of killing and murdering General Grant, and that Atzerodt knew that General Grant had left the city of Washington, a fact which is not disputed, on the Friday evening of the murder, by the evening train. Thus this intended victim of the conspiracy escaped, for that night, the knives and revolvers of Atzerodt, and O'Laughlin, and Payne, and Herold, and Booth, and John H. Surratt, and, perchance, Harper and Caldwell, and twenty others, who were then here lying in wait for his life.

In the mean time, Booth and Herold, taking the route before agreed upon, make directly after the assassination for the Anacostia bridge. Booth crosses first, gives his name, passes the guard, and is speedily followed by Herold. They make their way directly to Surrattsville, where Herold calls to Lloyd, "Bring out those things," showing that there had been communication between them and **Mrs. Surratt** after her return. Both the carbines being in readiness, according to Mary E. Surratt's directions, both were brought out. They took but one. Booth declined to carry the other, saying that his limb was broken. They then declared that they had murdered the President and the Secretary of State. They then make their way directly to the house of the prisoner Mudd, assured of safety and security. They arrived early in the morning before day, and no man knows at what hour they left. Herold rode towards Bryantown with Mudd about 3 o'clock that afternoon, in the vicinity of which place he parted with him, remaining in the swamp, and was afterwards seen returning the same afternoon in the direction of Mudd's house; about which time, a little before sundown, Mudd returned from Bryantown towards his home. This village at the time Mudd was in it was thronged with soldiers in pursuit of the murderers of the President, and although great care has been taken by the defence to deny that any one said in the presence of Dr. Mudd, either there or elsewhere on that day, who had committed this crime, yet it is in evidence by two witnesses, whose truthfulness no man questions, that upon Mudd's return to his own house, that afternoon, he stated that Booth was the murderer of the President, and Boyle the murderer of Secretary Seward, but took care to make the further remark that Booth had brothers, and he did not know which of them had done the act. When did Dr. Mudd learn that Booth had brothers? And what is still more pertinent to this inquiry, from whom did he learn that either John Wilkes Booth or any of his brothers had murdered the President? It is clear that Booth remained in his house until some time in the afternoon of Saturday; that Herold left the house alone, as one of the witnesses states, being seen to pass the window; that he alone of these two assassins was in the company of Dr. Mudd on his way to Bryantown. It does not appear when Herold returned to Mudd's house. It is a confession of Dr. Mudd himself, proven by one of the witnesses, that Booth left his house on crutches, and went in the direction of the swamp. How long he remained there, and what became of the horses which Booth and Herold rode to his house, and which were put into his stable, are facts nowhere disclosed by the evidence. The owners testify that they have never seen the horses since. The accused give no explanation of the matter, and when Herold and Booth were captured they had not these horses in their possession. How comes it that, on Mudd's return from Bryantown, on the evening of Saturday, in his conversation with Mr. Hardy and Mr. Farrell, the witnesses before referred to, he gave the name of Booth as the murderer of the President and that of Boyle as the murderer of Secretary Seward and his son, and carefully avoided intimating to either that Booth had come to his house early that day, and had remained there until the afternoon; that he left him in his house and had furnished him a razor with which Booth attempted to disguise himself by shaving off his moustache? How comes it, also, that, upon being asked by those two witnesses whether the Booth who killed the President was the one who had been there last fall, he answered that he did not know whether it was that man or one of his brothers, but he understood he had some brothers, and added, that if it was the Booth who was there last fall, *he knew that one*, but concealed the fact that this man had been at his house on that day and was then at his house, and had attempted, in his presence, to disguise his person? He was sorry, very sorry, that the thing had occurred, but not so sorry as to be willing to give any evidence to these two neighbors, who were manifestly honest and upright men, that the murderer had been harbored in his house all day, and was probably at that moment, as his own subsequent confession shows, lying concealed in his house or near by, subject to his call. This is the man who undertakes to show by his own declaration, offered in evidence against my protest, of what he said afterwards, on Sunday afternoon, the 16th, to his kinsman Dr. George D. Mudd, to whom he then stated that the assassination of the President was a most damnable act—a conclusion in which most men will agree with him, and to establish which his testimony was not needed. But it is to be remarked that this accused did not intimate that the man whom he knew the evening before was the murderer had found refuge in his house, had disguised his person, and sought concealment in the swamp upon the crutches which he had provided for him. Why did he conceal this fact from his kinsman? After the church services were over, however, in another conversation on their way home, he did tell Dr. George Mudd that two suspicious persons had been at his house, who had come there a little before daybreak on Saturday morning; that one of them had a broken leg, which he bandaged; that they got something to eat at his house; that they seemed to be laboring under more excitement than probably would result from the injury; that they said they came from Bryantown, and inquired the way to Parson Wilmer's; that while at his house one of them called for a razor and shaved himself. The witness says, "I do not remember whether he said that this party shaved off his whiskers or his moustache, but he altered somewhat, or probably materially, his features." Finally, the prisoner, Dr. Mudd, told this witness that he, in company with the younger of the two men, went down the road towards Bryantown in search of a vehicle to take the wounded man away from his house. How comes it that he concealed in this conversation the fact proved, that he went with Herold towards Bryantown and left Herold outside of the town? How comes it that in this second conversation, on Sunday, insisted upon here with such pertinacity as evidence for the defence, but which had never been called for by the prosecution, he concealed from his kinsman the fact which he had disclosed the day before to Hardy and Farrell, that it was

Booth who assassinated the President, and the fact which is now disclosed by his other confessions given in evidence for the prosecution, that it was Booth whom he had sheltered, concealed in his house, and aided to his hiding place in the swamp? He volunteers as evidence his further statement, however, to this witness, that on Sunday evening he requested the witness to state to the military authorities that two suspicious persons had been at his house, and see if anything could be made of it. He did not tell the witness what became of Herold, and where he parted with him on the way to Bryantown. How comes it that when he was in Bryantown on the Saturday evening before, when he knew that Booth was then at his house, and that Booth was the murderer of the President, he did not himself state it to the military authorities then in that village, as he well knew? It is difficult to see what kindled his suspicions on Sunday, if none were in his mind on Saturday, when he was in possession of the fact that Booth had murdered the President, and was then secreting and disguising himself in the prisoner's own house.

His conversation with Gardner on the same Sunday at the church is also introduced here to relieve him from the overwhelming evidences of his guilt. He communicates nothing to Gardner of the fact that Booth had been in his house; nothing of the fact that he knew the day before that Booth had murdered the President; nothing of the fact that Booth had disguised or attempted to disguise himself; nothing of the fact that he had gone with Booth's associate, Herold, in search of a vehicle, the more speedily to expedite their flight; nothing of the fact that Booth had found concealment in the woods and swamp near his house, upon the crutches which he had furnished him. He contents himself with merely stating "that we ought to raise immediately a home guard, to hunt up all suspicious persons passing through our section of country and arrest them, for there were two suspicious persons at my house yesterday morning."

It would have looked more like aiding justice and arresting felons if he had put in execution his project of a home guard on Saturday, and made it effective by the arrest of the man then in his house who had lodged with him last fall, with whom he had gone to purchase one of the very horses employed in this flight after the assassination, whom he had visited last winter in Washington, and to whom he had pointed out the very *route* by which he had escaped by way of his house, whom he had again visited on the 3d of last March, preparatory to the commission of this great crime, and who he knew, when he sheltered and concealed him in the woods on Saturday, was not merely a suspicious person, but was, in fact, the murderer and assassin of Abraham Lincoln. While I deem it my duty to say here, as I said before, when these declarations uttered by the accused on Sunday, the 16th, to Gardner and George D. Mudd, were attempted to be offered on the part of the accused, that they are in no sense evidence, and by the law were wholly inadmissible, yet I state it as my conviction that, being upon the record upon motion of the accused himself, so far as these declarations to Gardner and George D. Mudd go, they are additional indications of the guilt of the accused, in this, that they are manifestly suppressions of the truth and suggestions of falsehood and deception ; they are but the utterances and confessions of guilt.

To Lieutenant Lovett, Joshua Lloyd, and Simon Gavican, who, in pursuit of the murderer, visited his house on the 18th of April, the Tuesday after the murder, he denied positively, upon inquiry, that two men had passed his house, or had come to his house on the morning after the assassination. Two of these witnesses swear positively to his having made the denial, and the other says he hesitated to answer the question he put to him; all of them agree that he afterwards admitted that two men had been there, one of whom had a broken limb, which he had set; and when asked by this witness who that man was, he said he did not know—that the man was a stranger to him, and that the two had been there but a short time. Lloyd asked him if he had ever seen any of the parties, Booth, Herold and Surratt, and he said he had never seen them; while it is positively proved that he was acquainted with John H. Surratt, who had been in his house; that he knew Booth, and had introduced Booth to Surratt last winter. Afterwards, on Friday, the 21st, he admitted to Lloyd that he had been introduced to Booth last fall, and that this man, who came to his house on Saturday, the 15th, remained there from about 4 o'clock in the morning until about 4 in the afternoon; that one of them left his house on horseback, and the other walking. In the first conversation he denied ever having seen these men.

Colonel Wells also testifies that, in his conversation with Dr. Mudd on Friday, the 21st, the prisoner said that he had gone to Bryantown, or near Bryantown, to see some friends on Saturday, and that as he came back to his own house he saw the person he afterwards supposed to be Herold passing to the left of his house towards the barn, but that he did not see the other person at all after he left him in his own house, about 1 o'clock. If this statement be true, how did Dr. Mudd see the same person leave his house on crutches? He further stated to this witness that he returned to his own house about 4 o'clock in the afternoon; that he did not know this wounded man; said he could not recognize him from the photograph which is of record here, but admitted that he had met Booth some time in November, when he had some conversation with him *about lands* and horses; that Booth had remained with him that night in November, and on the next day had purchased a horse. He said he had not again seen Booth from the time of the introduction in November up to his arrival at his house on the Saturday morning after the assassination. Is not this a confession that he did see John Wilkes Booth on that morning at his house, and knew it was Booth? If he did not know him, how came he to make this statement to the witness: that "he had not seen Booth *after* November *prior* to his arrival there on the Saturday morning?"

He had said before to the same witness, he did not know the wounded man. He said further to Colonel Wells, that when he went up stairs after their arrival, he noticed that the person he *supposed* to be Booth had shaved off his moustache. Is it not inferable from this declaration that he *then* supposed him to be Booth? Yet he declared the same afternoon, and while Booth was in his own house, that Booth was the murderer of the President. One of the most remarkable statements made to this witness by the prisoner was that he heard for the first time on Sunday morning, or late in the evening of Saturday, that the President had been murdered! From whom did he hear it? The witness (Colonel Wells) volunteers his "impression" that Dr. Mudd had said he had heard it after the persons had left his house. If the "impression" of the witness thus volunteered is to be taken as evidence—and the counsel for the accused, judging from their manner, seem to think it ought to be—let this question be answered: how could Dr. Mudd have made that impression upon anybody truthfully, when it is proved by Farrell and Hardy that on his return from Bryantown, on Saturday afternoon, he not only stated that the President Mr. Seward and his son had been assassinated, but that Boyle had assassinated Mr. Seward, and Booth had assassinated the President? Add to this the fact that he said to this witness that he left his own house at 1 o'clock, and when he returned the men were gone, yet it is in evidence, by his own declarations, that Booth left his house at four o'clock on crutches, and he must have been there to have seen it, or he could not have known the fact.

Mr. Williams testifies that he was at Mudd's house on Tuesday, the

18th of April, when he said that strangers had *not* been that way, and also declared that he heard, *for the first time*, of the assassination of the President on Sunday morning, at church. Afterwards, on Friday, the 21st, Mr. Williams asked him concerning the men who had been at his house, one of whom had a broken limb, and he confessed they had been there. Upon being asked if they were Booth and Herold, he said they were not—*that he knew Booth.* I think it is fair to conclude that he did know Booth, when we consider the testimony of Weichmann, of Norton, of Evans, and all the testimony just referred to, wherein he declares, himself, that he not only knew him, but that he had lodged with him, and that he had himself gone with him when he purchased his horse from Gardner last fall, for the very purpose of aiding the flight of himself, or some of his confederates.

All these circumstances taken together, which, as we have seen upon high authority, are stronger as evidences of guilt than even direct testimony, leave no further room for argument, and no rational doubt that Doctor Samuel A. Mudd was as certainly in this conspiracy as were Booth and Herold, whom he sheltered and entertained; receiving them under cover of darkness on the morning after the assassination, concealing them throughout that day from the hand of offended justice, and aiding them, by every endeavor, to pursue their way successfully to their co-conspirator, Arnold, at Fortress Monroe, and in which direction they fled until overtaken and Booth was slain.

We next find Herold and his confederate Booth, after their departure from the house of Mudd, across the Potomac in the neighborhood of Port Conway, on Monday, the 24th of April, conveyed in a wagon. There Herold, in order to obtain the aid of Captain Jett, Ruggles, and Bainbridge, of the confederate army, said to Jett, "We are the assassinators of the President;" that this was his brother with him, who, with himself, belonged to A. P. Hill's corps; that his brother had been wounded at Petersburg; that their names were Boyd. He requested Jett and his rebel companions to take them out of the lines. After this Booth joined these parties, was placed on Ruggles's horse, and crossed the Rappahannock river. They then proceeded to the house of Garrett, in the neighborhood of Port Royal, and nearly midway between Washington city and Fortress Monroe, where they were to have joined Arnold. Before these rebel guides and guards parted with them, Herold confessed that they were travelling under assumed names—that his own name was Herold, and that the name of the wounded man was John Wilkes Booth, "who had killed the President." The rebels left Booth at Garrett's, where

Herold revisited him from time to time, until they were captured. At 2 o'clock on Wednesday morning, the 26th, a party of United States officers and soldiers surrounded Garrett's barn where Booth and Herold lay concealed, and demanded their surrender. Booth cursed Herold, calling him a coward, and bade him go, when Herold came out and surrendered himself, was taken into custody, and is now brought into court. The barn was then set on fire, when Booth sprang to his feet, amid the flames that were kindling about him, carbine in hand, and approached the door, seeking, by the flashing light of the fire, to find some new victim for his murderous hand, when he was shot, as he deserved to be, by Sergeant Corbett, in order to save his comrades from wounds or death by the hands of this desperate assassin. Upon his person was found the following bill of exchange:

"No. 1492. The Ontario Bank, Montreal Branch. Exchange for £61 12s. 10d. Montreal, 27th October, 1864. Sixty days after sight of this first of exchange, second and third of the same tenor and date, pay to the order of J. Wilkes Booth £61 12s. 10d. sterling, value received, and charge to the account of this office. H. Stanus, manager. To Messrs. Glynn, Mills & Co., London."

Thus fell, by the hands of one of the defenders of the republic, this hired assassin, who, for a price, murdered Abraham Lincoln, bearing upon his person, as this bill of exchange testifies, additional evidence of the fact that he had undertaken, in aid of the rebellion, this work of assassination by the hands of himself and his confederates, for such sum as the accredited agents of Jefferson Davis might pay him or them, out of the funds of the confederacy, which, as is in evidence, they had in "any amount" in Canada for the purpose of rewarding conspirators, spies, poisoners, and assassins, who might take service under their false commissions, and do the work of the incendiary and the murderer upon the lawful representatives of the American people, to whom had been intrusted the care of the republic, the maintenance of the Constitution, and the execution of the laws.

The court will remember that it is in the testimony of Merritt and Montgomery and Conover, that Thompson, and Sanders, and Clay, and Cleary, made their boasts that they had money in Canada for this very purpose. Nor is it to be overlooked or forgotten that the officers of the Ontario Bank at Montreal testify that during the current year of this conspiracy and assassination Jacob Thompson had on deposit in that bank the sum of six hundred and forty-nine thousand dollars, and that these deposits to the credit of Jacob Thompson accrued from the negotiation of bills of exchange drawn by the Secretary of the Treasury of the so-called Confederate States on Frazier, Trenholm & Co., of Liverpool, who were known to be the financial agents of the Confederate States. With an undrawn deposit in this bank of four hundred and fifty-five dollars, which has remained to his credit since October last, and with an unpaid bill of exchange drawn by the same bank upon London, in his possession and found upon his person, Booth ends his guilty career in this work of conspiracy and blood in April, 1865, as he began it in October, 1864, in combination with Jefferson Davis, Jacob Thompson, George N. Sanders, Clement C. Clay, William C. Cleary, Beverley Tucker, and other co-conspirators, making use of the money of the rebel confederation to aid in the execution and in the flight, bearing at the moment of his death upon his person their money, part of the price which they paid for his great crime, to aid him in its consummation, and secure him afterwards from arrest and the just penalty which by the law of God and the law of man is denounced against treasonable conspiracy and murder.

By all the testimony in the case it is, in my judgment, made as clear as any transaction can be shown by human testimony, that John Wilkes Booth and John H. Surratt, and the several accused, David E. Herold, George A. Atzerodt, Lewis Payne, Michael O'Laughlin, Edward Spangler, Samuel Arnold, Mary E. Surratt, and Samuel A. Mudd, did, with intent to aid the existing rebellion and to subvert the Constitution and laws of the United States, in the month of October last and thereafter, combine, confederate, and conspire with Jefferson Davis, George N. Sanders, Beverley Tucker, Jacob Thompson, William C. Cleary, Clement C. Clay, George Harper, George Young, and others unknown, to kill and murder, within the military department of Washington, and within the intrenched fortifications and military lines thereof, Abraham Lincoln, then President of the United States and commander-in-chief of the army and navy thereof; Andrew Johnson, Vice President of the United States; William H. Seward, Secretary of State; and Ulysses S. Grant, lieutenant general, in command of the armies of the United States; and that Jefferson Davis, the chief of this rebellion, was the instigator and procurer, through his accredited agents in Canada, of this treasonable conspiracy.

It is also submitted to the court, that it is clearly established by the testimony that John Wilkes Booth, in pursuance of this conspiracy, so entered into by him and the accused, did, on the night of the 14th of April, 1865, within the military department of Washington, and the intrenched fortifications and military lines thereof, and with the intent laid, inflict a mortal wound upon Abraham Lincoln, then President and Commander-in-chief of the army and navy of the United States, whereof he died; that in pursuance of the same conspiracy and within the said department and intrenched lines, Lewis Payne assaulted, with intent to kill and murder, William H. Seward, then Secretary of State of the United States; that George A. Atzerodt, in pursuance of the same conspiracy, and within the said department, laid in wait, with intent to kill and murder Andrew Johnson, then Vice President of the United States; that Michael O'Laughlin, within said department, and in pursuance of said conspiracy, laid in wait to kill and murder Ulysses S. Grant, then in command of the armies of the United States; and that Mary E. Surratt, David E. Herold, Samuel Arnold, Samuel A. Mudd, and Edward Spangler did encourage, aid, and abet the commission of said several acts in the prosecution of said conspiracy.

If this treasonable conspiracy has not been wholly executed; if the several executive officers of the United States and the commander of its armies, to kill and murder whom the said several accused thus confederated and conspired, have not each and all fallen by the hands of these conspirators, thereby leaving the people of the United States without a President or Vice President; without a Secretary of State, who alone is clothed with authority by the law to call an election to fill the vacancy, should any arise, in the offices of President and Vice President; and without a lawful commander of the armies of the republic, it is only because the conspirators were deterred by the vigilance and fidelity of the executive officers, whose lives were mercifully protected on that night of murder by the care of the Infinite Being who has thus far saved the republic and crowned its arms with victory.

If this conspiracy was thus entered into by the accused; if John Wilkes Booth did kill and murder Abraham Lincoln in pursuance thereof; if Lewis Payne did, in pursuance of said conspiracy, assault with intent to kill and murder William H. Seward, as stated, and if the several parties accused did commit the several acts alleged against them in the prosecution of said conspiracy, then, it is the law that all the parties to that conspiracy, whether present at the time of its execution or not, whether on trial before this court or not, are alike guilty of the several acts done by each in the execution of the common design. What these conspirators did in the execution of this conspiracy by the hand of one of their co-conspirators they did themselves; his act, done in the prosecution of the common design, was the act of all the parties to the treasonable combination, because done in execution and furtherance of their guilty and treasonable agreement.

As we have seen, this is the rule, whether all the conspirators are indicted or not; whether they are all on trial or not. "It is material what the nature of the indictment is, provided the offence involve a conspiracy. Upon indictment for murder, for instance, if it appear that others, together with the prisoner, conspired to perpetrate the crime, the act of one done in pursuance of that intention world be evidence against the rest." (1 Whar., 706.) To the same effect are the words of Chief Justice Marshall, before cited, that whoever leagued in a general conspiracy, performed any part, however MINUTE, or however REMOTE, from the scene of *action*, are guilty as principals. In this treasonable conspiracy, to aid the existing armed rebellion, by murdering the executive officers of the United States and the commander of its armies, all the parties to it must be held as principals, and the act of one in the prosecution of the common design the act of all.

I leave the decision of this dread issue with the court, to which alone it belongs. It is for you to say, upon your oaths, whether the accused are guilty.

I am not conscious that in this argument I have made any erroneous statement of the evidence, or drawn any erroneous conclusions; yet I pray the court, out of tender regard and jealous care for the rights of the accused, to see that no error of mine, if any there be, shall work them harm. The past services of the members of this honorable court give assurance that, without fear, favor, or affection, they will discharge with fidelity the duty enjoined upon them by their oaths. Whatever else may befall, I trust in God that in this, as in every other American court, the rights of the whole people will be respected, and that the Republic in this, its supreme hour of trial, will be true to itself and just to all—ready to protect the rights of the humblest, to redress every wrong, to avenge every crime, to vindicate the majesty of law, and to maintain inviolate the Constitution, whether assailed secretly or openly, by hosts armed with gold, or armed with steel.

www.ingramcontent.com/pod-product-compliance
Lightning Source LLC
Chambersburg PA
CBHW022141160426
43197CB00009B/1387